A Practical Guide to

Winning the War on Terrorism

HOOVER
NATIONAL
SECURITY
FORUM
SERIES

A Practical Guide to
Winning the War on Terrorism

EDITED BY

Adam Garfinkle

HOOVER INSTITUTION PRESS
Stanford University Stanford, California

www.hoover.org

Hoover Institution Press Publication No. 530
Copyright © 2004 by the Board of Trustees of the
  Leland Stanford Junior University

First printing 2004
10   09   08   07   06   05   04   9   8   7   6   5   4   3   2   1

Manufactured in the United States of America

The paper used in this publication meets the minimum requirements
of American National Standard for Information Sciences—Permanence
of Paper for Printed Library Materials, ANSI Z39.48-1992. ⊗

Library of Congress Cataloging-in-Publication Data
A practical guide to winning the war on terrorism / edited by Adam Garfinkle.
      p.   cm. — (Hoover national security forum series)
  Includes bibliographical references and index.
  ISBN 0-8179-4542-3 (alk. paper)
  1. Terrorism—Prevention.   2. War on Terrorism, 2001–
3. Terrorism—Government policy—United States.   4. United States—
Foreign relations—Middle East.   5. Islam and terrorism.   I. Garfinkle,
Adam M., 1951–   II. Series.
HV6431.P67   2004
303.6'25—dc22   2004002417

Contents

Authors

Lisa Anderson is dean of the School of International and Public Affairs at Columbia University. She has been on Columbia's faculty since 1986; prior to her appointment as dean, she served as chair of the Political Science Department and director of Columbia's Middle East Institute. She is author of *The State and Social Transformation in Tunisia and Libya, 1830–1980* (1986), coeditor of *The Origins of Arab Nationalism* (1991), editor of *Transitions to Democracy* (1999), and author of *Pursuing Truth, Exercising Power: Social Science and Public Policy in the Twenty-first Century* (2003).

In addition to her responsibilities at Columbia, Dean Anderson served as president of the Middle East Studies Association in 2003. She is also on the board of directors of Human Rights Watch, where she serves as cochair of the Middle East Advisory Committee. She is also chair of the Board of the Social Science Research Council.

Stephen Philip Cohen is a senior fellow in Foreign Policy Studies at the Brookings Institution. He was educated at the Universities of Chicago and Wisconsin and taught for many years at the University of Illinois. He has also served on the policy planning staff of the Department of State.

Dr. Cohen was the cofounder and chair of the workshop on Security, Technology and Arms Control for younger South Asian and Chinese strategists. He is the author or coauthor of ten books on Indian and Pakistani security policies and on American relations with the region. His most recent book is *The Idea of Pakistan and the Future of a Troubled State* (2004).

Michele Durocher Dunne is visiting assistant professor of Arabic language, linguistics, and literature at Georgetown University. She served in the Department of State from 1986–2003, including assignments as director of Near East Regional and North African Affairs at the National Security Council, on the secretary of state's policy planning staff, at the U.S. Embassy in Cairo, and at the U.S. Consulate General in Jerusalem.

Dr. Dunne holds a Ph.D. from Georgetown University in Arabic language and linguistics. She is the author of *Democracy in Contemporary Egyptian Political Discourse* (2003), which employs methods from linguistics and anthropology in a new approach to understanding political discourse in the Arab world.

Dale F. Eickelman, Ralph and Richard Lazarus Professor of Anthropology and Human Relations at Dartmouth College, has conducted extensive field research in North Africa and the Arabian Peninsula since the late 1960s. His recent books include *The Middle East and Central Asia: An Anthropological Approach*, 4th ed. (2002), and *Muslim Politics* (1996; new edition 2004), the latter of which was coauthored with James Piscatori.

In 2003, Indiana University Press published the second edition of *New Media in the Muslim World: The Emerging Public Sphere*, coedited with Jon W. Anderson, and in 2004, Brill will publish *Public Islam and the Common Good*, coedited with Armando Salvatore. Eickelman is also relationship coordinator for the American University of Kuwait–Dartmouth College project, which is the first English-language liberal arts university in Kuwait.

Graham E. Fuller, a former vice chair of the National Intelligence Council at the Central Intelligence Agency, has lived many years in different parts of the Muslim world. He also was a senior political scientist at RAND Corporation for twelve years. He is currently an independent writer and analyst and has written numerous books and articles about the Muslim world. His latest book is *The Future of Political Islam* (2003), which deals with the broader phenomenon of Islamist politics in a global context of developing world politics, including its terrorist aspects.

Adam Garfinkle is former editor of *The National Interest* and chief writer of the reports of the U.S. Commission on National Security/21st Century (the Hart-Rudman Commission). He has taught Middle East politics and U.S. foreign policy at the University of Pennsylvania, Haverford College, and the School of Advanced International Studies of the Johns Hopkins University. He was a research fellow at the Hoover Institution during 2003. The author of seven books and numerous essays, he is presently speechwriter to the secretary of state and a member of the Department of State's Policy Planning staff. *His work on and in this book reflects only his own views and does not represent the views of the U.S. government or the Department of State.*

F. Gregory Gause III is an associate professor of political science at the University of Vermont and director of the university's Middle East studies program. He was previously on the faculty of Columbia University (1987–1995) and was fellow for Arab and Islamic studies at the Council on Foreign Relations (1993–1994).

He is the author of two books, *Oil Monarchies: Domestic and Security Challenges in the Arab Gulf States* (1994) and *Saudi-Yemeni Relations: Domestic Structures and Foreign Influence* (1990). His recent articles on Saudi Arabian politics have appeared in *Foreign Affairs, World Policy Journal, Middle East Policy* and a number of edited volumes. He is currently working on a book project on the international politics of the Persian Gulf region since 1971.

His Royal Highness Prince El Hassan bin Talal has initiated, founded, and is actively involved in a large number of Jordanian and international institutes and committees. He is a founding member of the Parliament of Cultures, established in Istanbul in July 2003 to promote understanding among cultures of the world. His Royal Highness is currently working with several American nongovernmental organizations on a program called *Partners in Humanity,* the aim of which is to improve understanding and build positive relationships between the Muslim world and the United States.

Prince El Hassan is the author of eight books: *A Study on Jerusalem* (1979) (English); *Palestinian Self-Determination* (1981) (English, Arabic); *Search for Peace* (1984) (English, Arabic); *Christianity in the Arab World* (1994) (English, Arabic, French, Greek, Spanish, Russian, German); *Essere Musulmano* (coauthor, 2001) (Italian, French, Spanish, English); *Continuity, Innovation, and Change: Selected Essays* (2001) (English); *In Memory of Faisal I: The Iraqi Question* (2003) (Arabic); and *Q & A: Contemporary Issues* (2003) (Arabic).

M. A. Muqtedar Khan is a visiting fellow at Brookings Institution and director of International Studies at Adrian College. He is also a fellow of the Institute for Social Policy and Understanding and the present president of the Association of Muslim Social Scientists. He is the author of *American Muslims: Bridging Faith and Freedom* (2002) and *Jihad for Jerusalem: Identity and Strategy in International Politics* (2004).

Martin Kramer is editor of the Philadelphia-based *Middle East*

Quarterly. He is a senior associate (and past director) of the Moshe Dayan Center for Middle Eastern and African Studies at Tel Aviv University. He is also the Wexler-Fromer Fellow at The Washington Institute for Near East Policy. An authority on contemporary Islam and Arab politics, Dr. Kramer earned his undergraduate and doctoral degrees in Near Eastern Studies from Princeton University and another graduate degree from Columbia University. He has been a visiting professor at Brandeis University, the University of Chicago, Cornell University, and Georgetown University. On two occasions, Dr. Kramer has been a fellow of the Woodrow Wilson International Center for Scholars in Washington.

His authored and edited books include *Islam Assembled*; *Shi'ism, Resistance, and Revolution*; *Middle Eastern Lives*; *Arab Awakening and Islamic Revival*; *The Islamism Debate*; *The Jewish Discovery of Islam*; and *Ivory Towers on Sand: The Failure of Middle Eastern Studies in America.*

Daoud Kuttab is an award-winning Palestinian journalist and freedom-of-expression media activist. He is the director of the Institute of Modern Media at Al Quds University in Ramallah. He established Al Quds Educational Television, an independent voice for Palestinians. His work at Al Quds landed him in a Palestinian prison for broadcasting live a session of the Palestinian Legislative Council dealing with corruption.

He has won several media awards, among them awards from the New York–based Committee to Protect Journalists, the PEN Club, the International Press Institute, and the Leipzig Media Institute Award. He pioneered a number of progressive media projects, including AMIN.org, a Web site dedicated to posting uncensored Arab news and opinions, as well as AmmanNet.net, the Arab world's first independent Internet-based radio station. He was also the first Palestinian to conduct received his doctorate in Oriental studies (modern Middle Eastern history) from St. Antony's College, Oxford University.

Amir Taheri is the author of ten books on the Middle East and the Islamic world. He was executive editor of *Kayhan*, Iran's largest daily newspaper, from 1972–1979 and, for the past twenty-five years, has written for many Western and Middle Eastern publications on issues concerning the Muslim world. His syndicated columns appear in dozens of newspapers around the globe, including in many Muslim countries. His articles have appeared most recently in the *New York Times*, *Newsweek*, *Wall Street Journal*, *New York Post*, *Times of London*, and Canada's *National Post*, among many others.

Editor's Introduction

As virtually everyone is now prepared to admit, the problem of dealing with the threat of terrorism in an age of extant and potential weapons of mass destruction (WMD) proliferation is daunting. As conceived by the U.S. government, this problem, in practical policy terms, has two main parts: the military (or "kinetic," as it is called in the Pentagon) parts, and all the other parts.

The kinetic part is easily defined: using the military to kill terrorists "with a global reach," disrupt their infrastructure, and dissuade those who fund terrorists and their state sponsors upon threat (and occasionally actual visitation) of physical injury.

The nonkinetic parts are often euphemized as the "drain the swamp" or, better, the "hearts and minds" problem. These nonmilitary aspects focus on terrorism's motivation and recruitment patterns, the sociology of terrorist groups that leads them to mobilize, compete, and strike; and the underlying social conditions said to feed that motivation and those recruitment patterns.

The kinetic and nonkinetic aspects of the war on terrorism are clearly related. If a potential terrorist realizes that he will very likely fail in his political aims and stand a good chance of dying for his efforts, this, it may be presumed, will reduce his incentive to engage in terrorism.

However, the military side of the war against terrorism is only a necessary, not a sufficient, aspect of the solution. Weapons of mass destruction are activated by *ideas* of mass destruction, and these ideas arise from a complex of historical and social factors. Ideas of mass destruction, however, are not inevitable, and U.S. government policy can be formed to minimize their production and activation.

Such policy concerning the nonkinetic aspects of the war on terrorism is not a sidebar to the war on terrorism but a crucial part of it. If such actions are not taken, the military aspects of the war on terrorism could end up *increasing* the motivation for terrorism and recruitment into terrorist organizations. Clearly, while some potential terrorists will think better of bucking American power, others may be encouraged by some combination of personality traits, religious beliefs, and social context to *seek out* martyrdom in the face of a superior but alien power. This is why overthrowing the Taliban regime and eliminating a regime in Iraq with a long history of support for terrorism (if not specifically for al Qaeda) must be construed as merely a start in the war on terrorism—and not an entirely clear-cut start, at that. To recall Churchill's famous remark, these two campaigns may be "the end of the beginning," but they are unlikely to be seen in historical perspective as anything more than that.

Now, what about that social context? No honest observer can doubt that a range of social and political pathologies afflicts the Muslim and particularly the Arab world. This affliction is attested to most vividly by Muslims and Arabs themselves. Although the motivation for terrorism is obviously related to these pathologies, it is not identical to them. After all, these social pathologies existed *before* terrorism became a serious national security concern of the United States and its allies; so it follows that terrorism is *not* an inevitable by-product of such problems. Moreover, it will take generations to deal with the social and political problems of the greater Middle East, but dealing with mass-casualty terrorism cannot wait generations. For practical purposes, then, the problem of terrorism is separable, and must be separated, from the general issue of the social and political modernization of the Muslim and Arab worlds.

Getting at the nonkinetic aspects of the war on terrorism can be conceived as consisting of immediate, midterm, and long-term parts. The essence at all stages, however, appears to be fourfold:

1. Stigmatize the idea of murdering civilians for any political cause whatsoever, just as slavery, piracy, and human ritual sacrifice were so stigmatized in previous generations.

2. Identify and stop the flow of money and other resources at all levels from those who approve of terrorism to those who carry it out, redirecting that money and those resources to positive ends, as possible.

3. Refute, tirelessly and skillfully, the almost endless distortions of U.S. policies and motivations that are promulgated by Islamist propagandists (and others) and that inexorably make Americans and their allies targets of hatred and violence.

4. Work patiently at social, economic, and political reform (generally in that order) in Muslim-majority countries and among Muslim communities outside the Middle East and South Asia where terrorist cadres are known to have arisen.

The way U.S. and allied governments go about these basic tasks may involve many methods. One method has to do with persuasion and pressure at the private diplomatic level, especially as regards financial flows and other kinds of support for terrorism. This persuasion and pressure are where the kinetic and nonkinetic aspects of the war on terrorism have their most obvious relation. From the very start, the use of force, first in Afghanistan and then in Iraq, was designed to have both literal and demonstration effects. The demonstration effects were to flow from the literal effects, addressed to regimes such as those in Syria, Sudan, Libya, and Iran, for whom support for terrorism has been at some level not ideological but tactical and opportunistic. This method was one element of the Bush Doctrine, as it came to be called.[1]

At its inception, this intended demonstration effect was much maligned by critics. But look at what has happened. Sudan quickly turned state's evidence in private to the United States, and the significant progress made toward ending Sudan's civil war on reasonable terms owes much to the reduction of Khartoum's demands. In the background to the decisions made by the Sudanese government, there hovered implicitly an American "or else."

The Libyan decision in early March 2003 to do a dramatic about-face on support for terrorism and its WMD efforts looks to be another case in point of the diplomatic power of the American "or else." In this case, British and U.S. diplomacy played a major role in what deputy secretary of state Richard Armitage called "muscular multilateralism."

The Iranian decision to come at least partly clean on its own secret nuclear weapons program, as well as on its deliberate long-standing deception of the International Atomic Energy Agency (IAEA), seems to follow in train. Syria remains problematic in many ways, but grabbing al Qaeda operatives

---

1. See the remarks of Richard Perle, "After September 11: A Conversation," *The National Interest,* no. 65-S (Thanksgiving 2001): 84.

with $23 million and letting this be known, as happened in December 2003, can be interpreted as an insurance policy against being next on the list of an American axis of evil. Many in Washington hope that the regime in Pyongyang will get the message, too.

Power *is* important, and using it to win is *very* important. But much of what is required to win the war against terrorist recruiting and support cannot usefully be thought of as a spin-off of military efforts. Much of what is required is informational in nature. Some has to do with radio, television, and print media aimed at Muslim and Arab audiences. Some has to do with embassy outreach programs and related activities. Partnerships between government and nongovernmental organizations (NGOs), or outright private sector efforts, may make sense for many activities in which heavy and direct government participation may be unwise.

In all these methods, however, energy should be directed toward engaging and supporting religious, educational, intellectual, and cultural elites to stigmatize terrorism in ways that *resonate with indigenous values and metaphors*. The "brand America" method, which relies on Madison Avenue trope, will not work, because it too much reminds listeners of the materialist culture they tend to identify as the problem.

The purpose of this book is to aid in the development not only of general ideas but also of *practical steps* to undermine the fetid intellectual basis that sustains the grotesque notion that terrorism is a legitimate method of political struggle. We can disrupt and minimize recruitment patterns to terrorism organizations, and, less certainly and with more difficulty, we *can* affect the underlying conditions that lead some people to wander in such a direction.

To do so will take a major intellectual effort and then an equally serious effort to operationalize our knowledge. If it is to succeed, this effort cannot afford two types of vulgarity: that of anti-Muslim stereotyping and that of left-wing political correctness, where unpleasant truths may not be uttered in polite company. Such unfettered efforts are currently taking place in government, to be sure. Unfortunately, these efforts have not been making as much headway as even their champions would like, nor as much as they admit. They need and want help. The secretary of defense said so himself in his famous leaked "snowflake" of October 2003. This book is designed to be an answer, at least in part, to that snowflake, the full text of which is provided at the end of this introduction.

I want to acknowledge the support of the Hoover Institution and the encouragement of its director, John Raisian, in the development and publication of this book as part of its National Security Forum series. A debt of gratitude is also due Tod Lindberg, editor of *Policy Review* and a research fellow at the Hoover Institution, for his discerning editorial counsel. And, of course, I want to thank all the contributing authors who, despite already busy schedules, took the time to prepare essays for this volume.

Rather than put together a standard Hoover Institution collection of ten or twelve essays, each about 5,000 words in length, I have roughly doubled the number of essays and roughly halved their average length. I did this to involve a greater number of perspectives, for many perspectives are needed to do the subject justice. Moreover, as those who have worked in senior government positions know, principal decision makers do not typically read lengthy analytical discourses; they read memos. Therefore, I wanted the essays in this book to be closer to the literary form to which senior decision makers are accustomed, hoping to make it more likely that at least some decision makers will read them.

I also selected authors *all* of whom can work in at least one

Middle Eastern language and whose intimacy with the social settings and political cultures involved is beyond question. I did this, I confess, because of a lingering irritation. There has been a great and natural surge of interest in all things Middle Eastern and Islamic since September 11, 2001, and a horde of clever but often untutored journalists has risen to satisfy that interest. The results have not been particularly edifying. One simply cannot learn the nuances of the Middle East and of Islamic culture in a few days, weeks, or even months under the pressure of a magazine deadline. Those who think they can, or think they have actually done so, only illustrate how truly clueless they are: What they *do* know is so modest that they cannot fathom what they do *not* know. Thus, my decision as to author qualification is not no to journalists (there are some represented here), but rather no to amateurs.

I asked some authors to focus on the diplomatic aspects, some on media and information management, and some on educational and religious aspects of the problem. I asked some to focus on particular countries or questions. I asked all to consider immediate, midterm, and longer-term aspects of the problem. Most of all, I asked all authors to write as though they were addressing senior policy makers; I asked them to write crisply, to the point, and as specifically as the venue allowed. I also asked them to write quickly, so that we would not get stuck, as is so typical, in a drawn-out process that would render many ideas and proposals obsolete before their time.

I got some of what I asked for. But not every writer I invited accepted. Not all who accepted produced an essay. Not everyone was as crisp, as specific, and as quick as I had hoped. This has left some gaps, geographical and thematic, in the result. No essay focuses on Egypt or on Afghanistan, for example, which is unfortunate. Shutting down terrorist finances is not covered in as detailed a fashion as I had hoped, because little that one can say about this effort in public is worth saying, and what is worth saying cannot be said in public. The same goes for many aspects of intelligence and law-enforcement cooperation across borders.

There is more than I expected in the volume about public diplomacy; there is also more controversy over methods than I expected. The release of the Djerejian Report on public diplomacy, sponsored by secretary of state Colin L. Powell, after this project began but before it was completed, has only raised the prominence of the subject; but alas, obviously, for reasons of timing, the authors in this book were unable to attend fully to that report.[2]

I do not agree with everything said in this book, but I have seen my role as editor as that of intellectual impresario, not as censor. To use a sartorial metaphor, I have chosen the fabrics and defined the kinds of garments to be made, but I have neither crafted nor worn them.

I have also had a difficult time deciding on an order of presentation, not least because those who looked at specific countries did not leave off commenting more generally (which is good), and those who aimed to comment more generally sometimes invoked specific examples (which is also good). Though these are good traits, it makes for tremulous organization of the collection as a whole.

This does not disturb me, however, and it should not disturb you, dear reader. This book's imperfect cohesion reflects well, I think, where the country and the world are with regard to this problem: colloquially put, both are all over the place,

2. The formal title of this report is *Changing Minds, Winning Peace: A New Strategic Direction for U.S. Public Diplomacy in the Arab & Muslim World* (Washington, D.C.: Advisory Group on Public Diplomacy in the Muslim World, October 1, 2003).

which is *part* of the problem. (In any event, beyond this introduction, I decided to put my own two cents into this collection to make up for its frailties, to the extent I can.)

For all of the book's imperfections, the result is still a valuable one. The range and quality of the analyses, the sophistication of the disagreements, and the nuggets of specific proposals in this volume justify the effort exerted to produce it. Moreover, the fact that the collection works as a kind of political Rorschach test has a value of its own. Put this cluster of questions, as I did, before a group of experienced and intelligent men and women from America, Europe, and the Middle East, ask them to be practically minded and swift in their response, and this, exactly, is what you get. Years from now, perhaps, those wiser from experience than we are today will learn something just from that alone. One may hope so, anyway.

Adam Garfinkle
Washington, D.C.
December 25, 2003

TO: Gen. Dick Myers; Paul Wolfowitz; Gen. Pete Pace; Doug Feith
FROM: Donald Rumsfeld
SUBJECT: Global War on Terrorism

The questions I posed to combatant commanders this week were: Are we winning or losing the Global War on Terror? Is DoD changing fast enough to deal with the new 21st century security environment? Can a big institution change fast enough? Is the USG changing fast enough?

DoD has been organized, trained and equipped to fight big armies, navies and air forces. It is not possible to change DoD fast enough to successfully fight the global war on terror; an alternative might be to try to fashion a new institution, either within DoD or elsewhere—one that seamlessly focuses the capabilities of several departments and agencies on this key problem.

With respect to global terrorism, the record since September 11th seems to be:

- We are having mixed results with Al Qaida, although we have put considerable pressure on them—nonetheless, a great many remain at large.

- USG has made reasonable progress in capturing or killing the top 55 Iraqis.

- USG has made somewhat slower progress tracking down the Taliban—Omar, Hekmatyar, etc.

- With respect to the Ansar Al-Islam, we are just getting started.

Have we fashioned the right mix of rewards, amnesty, protection and confidence in the US?

Does DoD need to think through new ways to organize, train, equip and focus to deal with the global war on terror?

Are the changes we have and are making too modest and incremental? My impression is that we have not yet made truly bold moves, although we have made many sensible, logical moves in the right direction, but are they enough?

Today, we lack metrics to know if we are winning or losing the global war on terror. Are we capturing, killing or deterring and dissuading more terrorists every day than the madrassas and the radical clerics are recruiting, training and deploying against us?

Does the US need to fashion a broad, integrated plan to stop the next generation of terrorists? The US is putting relatively little effort into a long-range plan, but we are putting a great deal of effort into trying to stop terrorists. The cost-benefit ratio is against us! Our cost is billions against the terrorists' costs of millions.

- Do we need a new organization?
- How do we stop those who are financing the radical madrassa schools?
- Is our current situation such that "the harder we work, the behinder we get"?

It is pretty clear that the coalition can win in Afghanistan and Iraq in one way or another, but it will be a long, hard slog.

Does CIA need a new finding?

Should we create a private foundation to entice radical madrassas to a more moderate course?

What else should we be considering?

Please be prepared to discuss this at our meeting on Saturday or Monday.

Thanks.

Landscapes

1 Bush Is Right: Democracy Is the Answer

Amir Taheri

On April 9, 2003, Muslims throughout the world watched with a mixture of shock and awe as a statue of the Iraqi leader Saddam Hussein was pulled down in the center of Baghdad. Few may have regretted the fall of the statue. Islam bans images and icons as symbols of *shirk*, or pantheism—the gravest of sins in Muhammad's strict monotheistic vision. There is another reason few lamented the regime: Saddam's reign of terror had entered Islamic history as one of the blackest chapters of the postcolonial era.

So it is true that the Muslim world felt shock and awe, but not in the way the U.S. military intended. The actual feelings they felt and the reasons for those feelings need to be carefully understood.

Shock and Awe: The Real Thing

The shock and awe that many Muslims felt that April was real enough. It was as if the clock of history had been turned back to the early days of colonialism in the nineteenth century. For the first time in more than eight decades, Western armies were marching into the capital of a major Muslim state with the express mission of overthrowing its regime.

The entry of the American-led army into Baghdad had a far more dramatic effect than the Red Army's march into Kabul, the capital of Afghanistan, on Christmas Eve 1979. Back then, appearances had been preserved: a puppet Afghan regime had invited the Soviets to intervene, ostensibly to ward off attacks from Pakistan. In addition, most Muslims see Afghanistan as a wild realm—they call it "the land of insolence"—on the margins of Islam. Iraq, however, is regarded by many as the very heart of the Muslim world, recalling the "golden era" when Baghdad was the capital of an Islamic empire stretching from China to the Mediterranean Sea.

There was another reason for shock and awe. Whereas no one had seen the Soviet entry in Kabul on live television, the U.S.-led conquest of Baghdad, after just three weeks of what looked like an easy march from Kuwait, was broadcast live and watched by hundreds of millions of viewers.

The Muslim Debate

No one knows how long the shock-and-awe effect of Iraq's liberation may last in the Muslim world. What is certain is that the events of April 2003 could have an enduring effect on Muslims in general and Arabs in particular. What happened in Iraq could either work as a wake-up call to Muslims, especially Arabs, or serve as the leaven for a fresh bread of bitterness.

Both possibilities are present in the torrent of Arab and Muslim comment that preceded, accompanied, and followed the liberation of Iraq. There have been many calls on Arabs and Muslims in general to use the occasion for posing questions about their place in a world built and managed by "others." Some commentators have called on Muslims to adopt the cause of social, political, and economic reform and to attempt a long overdue *aggiornomento*.[1] Others have called for the opposite, demanding that Muslims close ranks, further distance themselves from the "alien world," and nurse their chagrin in the hope that, one day, Allah shall offer them an opportunity for revenge.[2]

A period of introspection and stocktaking may well be useful for both Muslims and the coalition of democracies led by the United States. Sooner or later, however, the two sides will have to enter into a dialogue to review their relations and work out a new modus vivendi.

What should that dialogue really be about?

In the year that preceded the American-led intervention in Iraq, the George W. Bush administration advanced a number of at times contradictory reasons and claims to justify the war. The main reason put forward in the diplomatic arena was that Hussein's regime had violated seventeen UN resolutions and was building an arsenal of forbidden weapons. Those reasons were, and remain, justified. But the principal reason for the U.S.-led intervention must be sought in the Bush administration's national security doctrine.

1. Among those who have sounded the wake-up call are such columnists as Turki al-Hamad, Abdul-Rahman al-Rashed, and Bakr Oweida among the Arabs and Ahmad Ahrar, Abdul-Karim Sorush, and Emadeddin Baqi in Iran.

2. The theme of a defensive wall has been hammered in by sympathizers of the now largely defunct al Qaeda terrorist organization, but it has received some support from more traditionalist Islamic thinkers, such as the Moroccan Muhammad Abed al-Jaberi.

Shaped in the aftermath of the September 11 attacks, the Bush Doctrine identifies global terrorism, sponsored or supported by "rogue states," as the principal threat to U.S. and global security. The analysis on which the doctrine is based asserts that only the dismantling of the rogue regimes and their replacement with democracies can once and for all remove the threat of global terrorism. That is because democracies do not sponsor terrorism, nor do democracies become bases of aggression against each other. Seen in that context, the regime change in Baghdad is only a first step on a long road that is to lead, first, to the establishment of a democratic system in Iraq and, then, to democratization throughout the Arab and Muslim worlds.

This, of course, is precisely what President Bush declared to be his goal in his November 6, 2003, speech at the National Endowment for Democracy. This goal constitutes a generational commitment to a vast program, one that is bound to go beyond President Bush's second term, provided he is reelected.

With few exceptions, the Muslim world, and the Arab countries in particular, represent an area of darkness as far as democratization is concerned. Few in the Muslim world have been touched by the historic changes that started with the fall of the Berlin Wall. Nor have many of them adapted well to the economic changes introduced under globalization since the 1990s. The Muslim world, representing some 18 percent of the planet's population, accounts for almost 70 percent of the globe's political prisoners and more than 80 percent of the world's political executions. Of the fifty-three predominantly Muslim countries, only two, Bangladesh and Turkey, hold reasonably fair elections that lead to orderly changes of government.

Most Muslim countries have also experienced economic

stagnation or decline in the past twenty years, as their demography has spiraled out of control. A by now well-known UN-sponsored report on human development in the Arab world, published in 2002, told a tale of woe about countries that, though endowed with immense natural resources, live close to starvation with little prospects of sustained development.[3]

To assert further that the Muslim world provides fertile ground for terrorism is an understatement. In at least thirty Muslim countries, terrorism, practiced either by the state or its opponents, is an integral part of political life. In several others, more classical forms of violence, including political murder, are used in the context of an often zoological struggle for power. A string of transnational terrorist groups enjoy varying degrees of support and maintain different types of logistical, financial, and training bases in a number of Muslim countries.

At the same time, the Muslim world really is the theater of what could be described as a civil war of ideas between modernizers, who preach democratization, and traditionalists, who urge Muslims to wall themselves in and adopt a defensive attitude toward what they regard as a hostile international system. Although this is not the first time this debate has been started, it is a peculiar debate this time around. For the first time in decades, perhaps a few centuries even, none of the Muslim countries can claim a leadership role and offer a coherent world vision. Traditionally, three Muslim countries—Iran, Turkey, and Egypt—have offered the Muslim world intellectual leadership in political and cultural fields. Today, however, none is in a position to do so.

Iran finds itself in an historic impasse under a discredited regime. Turkey has set aside its Muslim credentials in favor of

3. The UN Development Programme report on *Human Development in the Arab Countries*, 2002.

European ambitions shared even by the neo-Islamist coalition now in power. Egypt, under a septuagenarian dictator, has lost even its traditional audience in the Arab world. One other country that might have provided a measure of leadership is Saudi Arabia, but this kingdom is politically paralyzed under a geriatric leadership that has proved unable to shape a vision for its own country, let alone the Muslim world as a whole.

The Right American Role

Since the Muslims cannot drive their own debate to a useful conclusion, the United States must push them to do it—and it should, not least because the Bush administration's central thesis is correct: democratization is essential, not only for American security but also for social and economic development in the Muslim world. The question is how to bring about that democratization.

The Iraqi experience may or may not work, though I think it will. Provided the United States is prepared to stay the course, as it did in postwar Germany and Japan, President Bush's dream of transforming Iraq into a model of democracy for the Muslim world has a decent chance of success. But obviously, the United States cannot invade all Muslim states and occupy them long enough to establish democratic institutions, and the demonstration effect of a successful Iraqi democracy will not, by itself, be enough to reshape the region.

At the same time, the Muslim world simply cannot work its way out of the historic impasse in which it finds itself without outside help, at least not in the foreseeable future. In a sense, the Muslim world today resembles the Communist bloc in the late 1980s. Obvious differences notwithstanding, both exhibit a bankrupt ideology, corrupt elites, and economic decline—all combined with a growing desire at the base for opening to the West and seeking a share in the freedom and prosperity offered by the modern world. Perhaps this similarity offers a clue as to what to do.

Toward the end of the 1960s, the Western democracies decided to engage the Communist bloc in a network of relationships that went beyond the confrontational approach of the early Cold War. The new approach led to the diplomatic recognition of Communist China, the "opening to the East" exercise in Germany, and, more broadly, the policy of détente developed by the first Nixon administration.

A case could be made (and certainly was made) that these exercises merely prolonged the life of the Soviet bloc by providing it with economic aid, credit facilities, access to markets, and, perhaps more important, a presumption of moral equality with the West. Those who support that argument insist that the Soviet bloc ultimately collapsed because it could not meet the military, economic, and ethical challenge presented by a confrontational Reagan administration in the 1980s.

Many have considered the two trajectories of U.S. policy from the late 1960s to the late 1980s as contradictory. In retrospect, however, the two paths appear more as two phases of a dialectical movement. The policy of détente obliged the Soviet bloc to adhere to minimum rules of conduct that it might have otherwise rejected. Those rules promoted standards for behavior both inside and outside the bloc. The dissident movements could take shape without fear of executions and mass deportations, as had been the case in the Stalinist era. Advocates of change within the Soviet bloc knew that they were not alone and that the Western democracies regarded them as allies. The prospect of Soviet tanks again rolling into the capitals of Eastern Europe, as they had done in 1956 and 1968, receded. Reagan's confrontational approach succeeded partly because the Soviet bloc had become so dependent on the West in trade, economic, technological, and diplomatic terms and partly because, thanks to Western penetration of various kinds, the Kremlin lost its verve, its self-confidence, and its own sense of moral singularity.

Encore! Another Final Act

One key element of détente consisted of negotiations that led to the Helsinki Final Act of 1975. Though not a binding treaty, it was, in a sense perhaps, more important: It promulgated standards of behavior that could not be ignored. It took the political debate out of the ideological context, fixed by Marxist-Leninists, by emphasizing rules that would one day be claimed by Mikhail Gorbachev as "universal values." The question is: Can the Muslim world be engaged in a similar dialogue, leading to accords similar to those of the Helsinki Final Act?

The question merits consideration. Muslim states need political, social, and cultural reforms. They need to review their behavior at home and abroad. But few, even if they had the incentive, enjoy the legitimacy and the political strength to propose such reforms, let alone to implement them.

Nevertheless, all Muslim states are signatories to the Universal Declaration of Human Rights and to almost all the conventions drafted to implement it. It is no mystery, however, that almost all of those states violate the spirit and the letter of the declaration on a daily basis. It is important for the democratic world to insist that Muslim states honor their own signatures and respect their own commitments. Muslim states must be made to understand that there is a global public space regulated by international law that, though respectful of religious and cultural diversity, rejects transgression in the name of "alterity."

Committing the Muslim states to something like the Helsinki Final Act would be only the first step. The democracies also need to review their overall relations with the Muslim world, not least the political aspects of the West's high-end commercial relationships, especially with the Arabs.

For some major industrial nations, the Muslim world is nothing but a source of raw materials, notably oil, and a lucrative though distorted and lawless market. Some Western businesses, including major multinationals, have violated many rules when it comes to dealing with Muslim states. For example, Muslim states account for almost 27 percent of all arms purchases outside the NATO area. It is no mystery, too, that more than a thousand Western and Russian companies helped build Saddam Hussein's war machine, including his nuclear center of Osirak. As is well known, or ought to be, France built Osirak after Jacques Chirac, then prime minister, signed an agreement with Saddam Hussein, then vice president of Iraq, in 1975. There are striking photographs of that day that make for most interesting viewing.

Muslim despots are very much encouraged by the lack of courage that some Western governments show in attempting to defend and promote democratic values and human rights. The European Union, for example, has agreed to change the label it uses for talks with Iran from "critical dialogue" to "comprehensive dialogue" to please the mullahs, who believe they are above criticism. Although the EU has feigned toughness in dealing with the Iranian nuclear weapons program, it refuses to call obvious Iranian violations of the Nonproliferation Treaty what they are. The EU also refuses to seriously hold up the implementation of trade arrangements over the matter. The EU's view toward the Iranian mullahs closely resembles the fellow who keeps feeding carrot soup to a lion in the belief that the lion will eventually become a vegetarian.

Unrolling the red carpet for despots, including those open to charges of crimes against humanity, and visiting them in their capitals to pay respect are other signs of European cowardice when it comes to upholding the values that provided the backbone of the Helsinki Final Act.

This is not an entirely new idea, by the way. Committing the Muslim nations to common standards of behavior was one of the goals pursued by the late Malaysian prime minister Tunku Abdul Rahman, who subsequently became secretary-general of the Islamic Conference Organization. In 1970, Abdul Rahman circulated the text of a proposed charter that spelled out an "Islamic understanding" of human rights and that committed the Muslim states to a wide range of reforms. The proposed charter envisaged the nonrecognition of regimes created through military coups d'état and sanctions against governments found guilty of violating the basic rights of citizens. The proposal went nowhere because most Muslim states saw the risks as too high and the rewards as illusory.

Turgut Özal, then Turkey's prime minister, made a similar proposal in 1986. But he, too, achieved little success because his call for reform was not backed by economic and military power.

Since then, various Muslim states have committed themselves to similar standards of behavior by joining a variety of regional groupings that include Western and other non-Muslim powers. These groupings include the Barcelona process and the Asia-Pacific summit. In addition, the EU has concluded bilateral accords with a number of Muslim states. It is important now *to link all those accords and reinforce them in the form of a single memorandum of understanding between the Muslim world and the major democratic powers.* Such a memorandum would provide the terms of reference that the democratic world could use to provide moral and material support for the growing reform movements in the Muslim world. Military action against some despotic regimes may still be necessary, but the idea that the Muslim world could be democratized through military invasion and occupation, on the Iraqi model, is unrealistic, to say the least.

In most Muslim countries today, there are identifiable democratic forces that the major democracies must support. Establishing contacts with thousands of nongovernmental organizations in the context of a people-to-people relationship will enable the democracies to help strengthen civil society in many Muslim countries. The time to pursue these goals is now.

This scenario *is* possible. Everyone who cares about this subject, which, after all, will define much about our future, must realize that the debate between the Muslim world and the democracies is not a theological one. Whatever version of Islam may be in the ascendancy in the Muslim world at present is irrelevant to the purpose at hand. People are, and ought to be, free to believe whatever they like. What concerns the rest of the world is the effect of any set of beliefs on the international public space. And there lies the problem. The Muslim world is sinking in economic failure, political despotism, cultural turpitude, and social crisis—all of which produce violence and terrorism. To emerge from this quagmire, Muslim states need a helping hand. It is in the best interests of the democracies to offer that helping hand. No time like the present.

2 | Terrorism: Sources and Cures

Graham E. Fuller

Terrorism is a method of political struggle or warfare available to any player, including individuals, groups, and states. Its history is as old as human conflict. Yet terrorism has taken on greater salience with the increasing ability of small groups to employ ever more dangerous and lethal forms of attack against the public or the state.

Furthermore, terrorism is a great equalizer of power. It is, colloquially put, the poor man's weapon. Not surprisingly, great powers tend to be far more distressed at the potential equalization of power afforded by terrorism than are small powers. This was clearly demonstrated when the United States was itself targeted by terrorism; only then did the U.S. government define terrorism as a serious global problem. Before terrorism was directly targeted against its own homeland, Washington did not consider it a serious problem, even though many other countries had suffered such attacks for decades.

In addition, America's international strategy under the Bush administration has increased both the profile and the problem posed by terrorism. Dominated by a neoconservative philosophy and a strategic global vision of unparalleled ambition to remake the world, U.S. policy has, ironically, increasingly become a lightning rod for global terrorism, propagating the "global" nature of the problem. This increase has become even more evident as American soldiers on patrol in Iraq can now be attacked by foreign guerrillas on a more level playing field than ever before.

In short, terrorism is, and has always been, a problem; but it is the victimization of the United States itself, which sits atop the international power hierarchy, that has made terrorism a more prominent and pressing issue. The reaction of the United States in launching the global war on terrorism has raised the profile of the terrorism issue to unprecedented heights, so that it now dominates most aspects of the Bush administration's foreign policy.

Problems of Definition

Analyses of terrorism—and ascriptions as to its causes and remedies—are hampered by an absence of any agreed-upon definitions. As a consequence, casual and arbitrary invocations of the term *terrorism* tend to serve the interests of the speaker. Those who possess the power to define the problem are well positioned to define the solution, even when there is considerable disagreement on the matter.

Nonetheless, at a minimum, most observers would agree that terrorism involves attacks against "innocent" civilians and noncombatants in the fulfillment of political goals. Many insist that terrorism, by definition, can be conducted only by nonstate actors, but a serious treatment of the phenomenon cannot exclude the use of "terror" by the state itself against its own or other citizens. In this case, the broader definition is better: the failure to include terror perpetrated by the state exculpates the state from what may be one primary cause of terrorism.

Westerners socialized into certain articles of faith about the nature of the Western state have trouble accepting the idea that the state itself could be capable of terrorism. Specifically, we learn from Weberian traditions that the state, by definition, has a "monopoly over the legal use of violence." Such a definition enjoys understandable resonance in the West precisely because most Western states represent the will of the public as expressed in free elections. Electorates have the ability to remove unwanted or dangerous leaders. The democratic state is expected to act in a fair and impartial way and hence should be the sole instrument entrusted with the use of violence against its own citizens.

In most of the rest of the world, however, regimes are not elected, lack basic democratic legitimacy, cannot be removed by the public at large, and routinely employ forms of intimidation and terrorist brutality to maintain a monopoly of political power. The terrors of the Stalinist, fascist, and Maoist state are obvious historical examples. Beleaguered populations often turn to violence or terrorism as a response to the illegitimate and repressive state.

Thus, a key psychological notion lies behind much of the perception and use of terror: terrorism is often seen in the developing world to be more "justified," or at least less morally reprehensible, when the weak use it against the strong as their main, or only, weapon of resistance. Ironically, contemporary values of human rights and democracy, and concepts of national self-determination and social justice, may have stimulated the use of terror among oppressed or frustrated groups in a misguided search for "justice" on the international and national level. Many oppressed peoples used to take their condition for granted; they no longer do.

In addition, for both descriptive and policy purposes, analysts of terrorism distinguish among *types* of terrorism. One important basic distinction concerns the dimensions and specificity of the group's goals. Groups with millenarian, apocalyptic goals with global ambitions (al Qaeda, Aum Shinrikyo, Baader-Meinhof, and such) differ from those with regional, local, and finite goals (usually nationalist goals, such as those of Chechens, Palestinians, Tamil Tigers, Basques, and so on). The limited and concrete goals and grievances of some groups can be negotiated—even resolved—in ways that millenarian goals cannot.

Of course, discussion of the *causes* of terrorism can never justify reversion to terrorism. However, discussion can suggest possible lines of approach to try to lessen terrorism. Modern societies, after all, *do* legally treat quite differently the various ways in which human lives are taken, distinguishing among first- and second-degree murder, manslaughter, criminal negligence, and capital punishment.

Nor does the existence of genuine grievances automatically lead to terrorism: Witness the deplorable conditions extant in much of Africa, where indigenous terrorism directed against the state is rare. The state in Africa is weak, however, making guerrilla war from the bush more effective than terrorism against a pudgy state. In Latin America, anti-U.S. terror was at one time widespread, but is currently minimal. This change has to do partly with the democratization of governance across most of the region.

Looked at side by side, the two examples of Africa and Latin America teach us something important: terrorism is ineffectual when the state is transparent, and it is unnecessary and unsustainable when the state is democratic. This brings us to the Muslim and particularly the Arab world, where states are, in the main, neither transparent nor democratic.

Definitions Applied

There is no doubt that today the Muslim world is the primary source and locus of terrorism. The reasons for this are complex and can be long debated, but the very existence of a vast "Muslim world" is itself one factor. In today's wired world, the international community of Muslims—the *umma*—is exquisitely attuned to the grievances of Muslims everywhere. Muslims can directly identify with the problems of other Muslims and are inclined to see themselves as a civilization under siege on a global level.

The echo chamber effect of the wired *umma*—reinforcing a sense of collective grievance—is a distinctive feature not found in other violent cultures around the world. Africans, for example, rarely speak with a common African voice about "African grievances," even in very violent cultures.

Many more reasons can be adduced to help explain—*but not explain away*—the salience of terrorism in the contemporary Muslim world: a millennium or more of periodic geopolitical clashes between various European forces and their most immediate cultural neighbor (the Muslim world); the historical uniqueness of the founding of the state of Israel, populated by people coming mostly from Europe on territory that was seen as inherently Muslim; and the high economic stakes swirling around vital energy resources that have facilitated a history of Western intervention in the Muslim world. And finally, we have the pervasiveness of authoritarian rule, sometimes facilitated, sometimes merely tolerated, by U.S. policies. A Muslim sense of helplessness, cynicism, frustration, and impotence in being unable to change any feature of domestic repression, or to affect the international forces that bolster that domestic order, clearly contributes to radical and violent responses.

The phenomenon of national liberation movements among Muslim minorities seeking freedom from harsh non-Muslim rule is especially important at the local level: Bosnians, Palestinians, Kosovars, Chechens, Kashmiris, Uighurs, Moros, and others all have turned to local violence in struggles that eventually become internationalized into yet another "Muslim cause." (Note that *intra-Muslim* separatist movements, such as those of the Kurds in Turkey or the Berbers in Algeria, do not fall into the category of "Muslim causes" and are also more amenable to solution.) These cases of local terrorism are quite distant from the phenomenon of al Qaeda, even if there is some incidental or opportunistic interaction. In this context, the crucial distinction between terrorism (against civilians) and guerrilla war (against authority) becomes vital. All terrorists are unprivileged combatants according to international law, wearing neither uniform nor insignia, but not all unprivileged combatants are terrorists.

The grievances, challenges, and conflicts of the Middle East are, of course, not new. They all long precede the modern phenomenon of international terrorism in the name of Islam. Yet grievances always find vehicles for expression, and today it is Islam, or Islamism, that serves as a vehicle for grievances and aspirations earlier expressed by Arab nationalism or Marxism-Leninism. Indeed, Palestinian terrorism has gone through each of these iterations in which one and then another ideology was adopted as a vehicle and later cast off. But all were aimed at achieving the same thing: an independent Palestinian state. In Uzbekistan, Islam was all but dead after seventy years of Communist repression. However, within less than a decade after independence, Islam became the vehicle of choice for combating a new, neo-Stalinist "national" Uzbek regime.

The success of the Islamist *mujahideen* in their jihad in Afghanistan against Soviet occupation lent special adrenaline to the Islamist cause, demonstrating that Islamism could even defeat a superpower (with a little help from U.S. arms). In other words, a disparate collection of local Muslim grievances has come to be reconfigured into one grander, more resonant, more global, and "civilizational" cause. These accumulated regional grievances—some legitimate, others ambiguous, a few fanciful—reached a head in the horrific events of September 11. Does that event represent a watershed, a high point of terrorism in international politics, or is it merely the most dramatic early expression in what may be an era of ongoing terrorist violence?

What Is to Be Done?

The answer to the question of what is to be done matters, because it should size and define the U.S. response. The trouble is, the answer is not obvious.

After the drama of September 11, the U.S. government made a good beginning at harnessing the moral indignation of the world to work in greater concert against *international* terrorism. Important progress has been made in identifying individuals, their modus operandi, and their mechanisms of travel and funding. New counterterrorism measures have immensely complicated the task of the terrorist, even if these measures may never completely eliminate terrorism. (This is another reason for treating terrorism as crime and not war: war comes to an end, but crime does not.) This kind of international cooperation needs to be enhanced and deepened, routinized and institutionalized.

International terrorist movements, as proclaimed by the Bush administration, should be the primary target of such global cooperation, but what constitutes "international" is in part a political judgment. Are locally based movements with local goals that nevertheless maintain international contacts part of international terrorism?

If we do not maintain the distinction, we risk stoking the kind of terrorism most dangerous to us. One of the major failings of the Bush administration's global war on terrorism (GWOT) is that it is too expansively defined, permitting nearly all dictators and regimes to embrace it and to declare their own local opponents all to be terrorists—and hence legitimate targets of the larger antiterrorism struggle. In effect, the GWOT has given license to many nasty regimes to depoliticize and then criminalize any local resistance and ethnic movements that have recourse to political violence—and this in countries where nearly all resistance to the state is treated violently. Across the globe, states like Russia, China, Israel, India, Egypt, Algeria, Tunisia, the Philippines, and others have exploited the GWOT for their own ends, and in so doing, they have usually increased internal repression. In most of these cases, the criminalization of legitimate political grievances has worsened the problem, heightened tensions, and intensified anti-American feeling.

In the Middle East, the problems associated with this dynamic are particularly complex and problematic. Few regimes in that area are legitimate in terms of popular support and electoral legitimacy. Until legal channels exist for the expression of grievances—often not just by minorities but also by the majority of the population against unpopular authoritarian regimes—there will be latent sympathy for acts of violence against the repressive state.

Of course, nearly all Muslims are aware that true acts of terrorism are criminal and violate the principles of Islam, but because of widespread anger against regimes, or against U.S. interventionism, these acts are rationalized as understandable and hence justifiable in some way. This very mood of frustration, anger, helplessness, and impotence creates a social environment of acquiescence toward many terrorist acts, especially those of an anti-American or antiregime nature. There will be no serious progress against terrorism until this environment of social permissiveness toward terrorism is altered. Unfortunately, force is the least effective tool in altering this mood of permissiveness and acquiescence.

How might terrorism come to be perceived differently by society in ways that will facilitate its disappearance? The United States itself might be a hypothetical case in point.

The bombing in Oklahoma City was condemned by nearly all Americans as an outrage, without qualification. But suppose such an incident had been perpetrated in the 1960s by African Americans? There would, of course, have been widespread condemnation of the act, but there would have been plenty of "buts," just as there were in discussing race riots in Watts, Detroit, and other places. Many Americans, while condemning the act, might have reasoned that the event was not surprising given social conditions among African Americans. Many African Americans would have felt considerable ambivalence about such an act.

This hypothetical case resembles the attitudes of most Muslims today toward terror against the United States and against repressive regional regimes: awareness that it is wrong, and against Islam, "but . . . ." This socially sanctioned "but" will be altered only when the broad public perceives that such an act is unjustifiable by *any* standard and that the cost to society from such acts is unacceptably high.

Punishment visited from abroad, as in the GWOT, may impose high costs upon Muslim societies, but it is unlikely to carry moral persuasiveness. It is more likely to touch off counterproductive consequences elsewhere. In realistic terms, a broad social reaction across the Muslim world against terrorism will regrettably be a long time in coming, at least in a number of societies where conditions are especially conducive to frustration and violence. To be successful, that type of reaction will require action by *elected Muslim leaders* who enjoy the legitimacy to move against such criminal acts. Leaders lacking this legitimacy will find limited popular support in crushing perpetrators of political violence. Chechen, Kashmiri, and Palestinian leaders, for example, will enjoy popular support in stamping out terrorist action from within their ranks *only* when the public at large feels that such acts are not only against religious principles, but also no longer justifiable because they are unnecessary in light of the ascent of legitimate state power.

The United States thus needs to combine reformist and punitive measures in meeting this complex challenge. As to the latter, the failure of the United States to respond to attack, or to those regimes that abet and encourage attack, would display a dangerous weakness. But punitive measures have little demonstration effect, so they should be used only when absolutely necessary. Even more than punitive measures, we need to engage in both conflict resolution and the promotion of genuine institutional reform abroad.

Local grievances that breed violence, though complex, are manageable, particularly when combined with the legitimizing weight of international cooperation as opposed to unpopular unilateral action. When local grievances are dealt with, local actors will be less drawn to the "internationalization" of diverse and abstruse "Muslim causes." Nonlocal millenarian terrorists will then find a much more limited pool of recruits available for their quixotic causes and a much greater local willingness to deal with such terrorists harshly.

In addition, we must work to reduce the number of non-democratic regimes that repress and terrorize their own people, thereby giving rise to the legitimation of apocalyptic terrorist responses. That is a very difficult task, and, regrettably, we are a long way from achieving it right now. President Bush has recognized this facet of the problem, notably in his November 6, 2003 speech at the National Endowment of Democracy. But whether the administration, or its successors, can match wise action to soaring rhetoric in a serious way remains to be seen.

This analytic framework will not satisfy a policy maker looking for a quick and efficacious way to win the war against terror. There is no such way. Heightened police work and international cooperation can make international terrorism more manageable, but as long as radical conditions and grievances exist, especially in the special conditions of the Muslim world, radical vehicles to express them will be found. If the "solution" to the problem of terrorism will be long in coming, let's remember that the problem that exploded on September 11 was a long time in coming, too.

3 | Liberalism and the War on Terrorism

Lisa Anderson

The events of September 11 focused minds around the world in a dreadful way. Suddenly, terrorism, which has always been ghastly, seemed immensely powerful. The whole world seemed to stop in its tracks, stunned by the audacity, the damage, the anger that the events of the day represented. The government of the most powerful country in the world seemed bewildered—almost unhinged—by the attack. Within hours, the Bush administration concentrated its attention on military responses. The U.S. government's construction of the attack not as a crime but an act of war met very little opposition, at least among Americans, and it justified a massive military effort, first against Afghanistan and then, less directly, in Iraq.

This accent on force was neither the only policy response available at the time nor is it the only option open to the United States today. There was, from the outset, a minority opinion—within and, more vocally, outside the government—that advocated a multilateral policing operation, framed by international law. Typically, this position was associated with an emphasis on a limited military response and a refusal to credit the authors of the attacks with the sort of influence in the Muslim world both they and the Bush administration seemed to accord them. It also rested on a conviction that the attacks—indeed, the very appearance of al Qaeda and other Islamist movements—were indications of deeper problems whose solution would require a broad-based and multifaceted approach.

Until the aftermath of the war in Iraq, the Bush administration evinced little interest in this line of argument. Having taken office declaring that "we don't do nation-building," the president and his advisers approached the challenge of September 11 less as the symptom of a systemic or organic problem in the Middle East and more as what might be called—with apologies to Durkheim—a mechanical puzzle. That is, they appeared to believe that by unseating a couple of already unpopular governments (say, Afghanistan and Iraq), intimidating a few others, rounding up several thousand people who might have connections with al Qaeda, monitoring illicit transfers of money, and tightening up visa procedures, they would have the problem under control, perhaps even solved.

However, attacks on Americans increased rather than declined as these measures were taken—largely, of course, because these measures put more Americans directly in harm's way in Iraq and Afghanistan. Whether recruitment to groups espousing anti-American aims actually increased worldwide as a result of the administration's conduct of its war on terrorism is impossible to know, but it is certainly plausible. In any event, the Bush administration was soon forced to concede that something very like nation-building—or more accurately, state-building—was indeed on the agenda.

Rather than simply trumpet "I told you so," those who

argued earlier for a more inclusive and multipronged response should now seize this new opportunity. Instead of castigating the misguided architects of the war on terrorism, all of us who care both about the well-being of Americans and the security and prosperity of the rest of the world—indeed, who believe the two may be linked—should consider the nature of the deeper troubles that spawned the attacks and the U.S. policies that might constructively contribute to addressing them.

Three Considerations, Three Tasks

At least three features of such a consideration are important. First, as suggested, it is not actually *nations* that we should contemplate helping to build but states and civil governments. Second, taking seriously the efforts to construct such institutions abroad will demand that we be more faithful to our own institutions at home and to the values they represent. Finally, we must think seriously about how we choose our prospective partners in these projects of reconstruction and development. Let me take each of these points in turn.

The distinction between nations, on one hand, and states and civil governments, on the other, points to the difference between those elements of our social lives that reflect personal identity—language, ethnic attachments, religious affiliations, national identity—and those constructed to allow us to enjoy those attachments and identities undisturbed. The United States has no business building, or even helping to build, nations or ethnic groups or religions. But there may be something to be said for assisting in building states, or better still, commonwealths—societies of people, as John Locke put it in his justly famous 1689 *Letter Concerning Toleration*, "constituted only for the procuring, preserving and advancing of their civil interests." By "civil interests," Locke intended "life, liberty, health and indolency of body; and the possession of outward things, such as money, lands, houses, furniture, and the like." In other words, it is the responsibility of governments to preserve and protect the rights to life, liberty, and the pursuit of happiness.

These are the ideas and values that underlie such policies as democracy promotion, advocacy of the rule of law, governance programs, and human rights monitoring. They are all, in their own way, efforts to instill respect for the liberal institutions that permit individuals and communities to enjoy their personal affections and private attachments in peace. Far too often in U.S. policy circles, these programs have seemed expendable in, or even detrimental to, our pursuit of other purposes, such as economic development or, more often, military security. Yet, if nothing else, the attacks of September 11 demonstrate that, in this global era, neither personal security nor collective prosperity—our treasured "life, liberty, and the pursuit of happiness"— are secure in the absence of the institutions that procure, preserve, and advance such interests around the world.

By no coincidence at all, Locke's argument should sound very familiar to Americans—it is the bedrock of our liberal tradition, codified in our very own Bill of Rights. It says nothing about language or ethnicity, nationalism, or, most important, religious preference. Indeed, Locke's whole purpose was to "distinguish exactly the business of civil government from that of religion."

To uphold this attachment to the civil government of a commonwealth may be difficult in the face of the taunting religious rationales that the authors of the attacks of September 11 offered. Yet the temptation to respond in kind must be energetically resisted.The Bush administration's reaction— not simply in President George W. Bush's initial reference to a "crusade" against this enemy but in the moral justification of the war on terrorism as a "righteous cause" against an enemy that is "absolutely evil"— conveyed a message that is deeply antithetical to the liberal purposes of what might be called commonwealth-building. The Bush administration's enthusiasm for "faith-based initiatives," whether in war or welfare, cannot privilege religious commitments—of any kind—over the preservation of liberal rights without distorting and confusing the purposes of the United States in the world.

Moreover, America will not be able to advocate effectively for institutions based on liberal rights abroad if we are not scrupulous in their observance at home. Obviously, terrorists have little sympathy with a world in which the process of arriving at a conclusion—electoral competition, for example, or trial by jury—is as important as the conclusion itself—a new government or policy, a determination of guilt or innocence. In the face of the insult and injury of the attacks of September 11, some Americans have been tempted to follow suit, suspending adherence to conventional procedures and declaring a virtual state of emergency in which virtuous ends excuse deplorable means.

The temptation to cheat to win is a powerful one, particularly when confronting an enemy that seems to know no restraint. But ultimately, what is true of terrorism is also true of the response: certain means are never justified, no matter what the end. We cannot compromise our commitment to the rule of law and remain either the society for which we are fighting or a society we will be able to persuade others to emulate.

Commonwealth-building thus entails two sets of demands—those we make on ourselves and those we may make on others. We cannot bend the law at home—creating novel classifications of convenience like "unlawful combatants" for terrorist suspects, according them the rights of neither criminal suspects nor prisoners of war. If we evade the recognized standards of the laws of war, for example, or suspend habeas corpus to hold individuals suspected of terrorist attachments without trial for months, we cannot expect others to observe the rule of law elsewhere.

Let us imagine for a moment that we do succeed in meeting our own high standards. If we were to regain our equilibrium and acknowledge the foundational importance of the liberal values embedded in both our own Constitution and in many of the international institutions to which our deference has long been far too cavalier, such as the Universal Declaration of Human Rights, with whom would we talk in the Middle East or the Muslim world?

It is certainly not self-evident to most Americans, including policy makers, that the region in which Osama bin Laden and his confederates cavort, stretching from Morocco to Afghanistan or even Indonesia, is home to many liberals. Certainly, the area's many admirers of bin Laden, who celebrate his ability to upset the world's last superpower, to threaten local governments around the region, and to divide the free world against itself, are not liberals. Nor, it must be said, are any of the region's governments, whatever lip service they may pay to liberalism whenever Congress is considering next year's foreign and military aid authorizations.

Yet there are increasingly vocal, articulate voices in the region itself—people who are refusing to let their societies sink into a war between the illiberal tyranny of the regimes and the nihilist anarchy of the opposition. These will be our true allies in building commonwealths.

Note that I said allies, not collaborators or instruments. Listen to the authors of the *Arab Human Development Report*:

The only way to meet the challenge [in Iraq] is to enable the Iraqi people to exercise their basic rights in accordance with international law, free themselves from occupation, recover their wealth, under a system of good governance representing the Iraqi people and take charge of rebuilding their country from a human development perspective.

This is the voice of people who share the values Locke articulated, arguing for a vision, as they put it, "guaranteeing the key freedoms of opinion, speech and assembly through good governance bounded by the law." So, yes, there are liberals in the Middle East. They are prominent academics, journalists, NGO activists, business consultants, international organization representatives, even the occasional government minister or parliamentarian. Rather than ignore them, portraying the battle in the region as one simply between friendly, pliant governments and divisive, dangerous oppositions or, even worse, between absolute and singular incarnations of good and evil, we should listen for, and indeed amplify, these voices.

Perhaps unsurprisingly, the liberal authors of the *Arab Human Development Report* also exhibit an attachment to self-reliance that most Americans would certainly recognize and celebrate in themselves. Anyone who has ever tried to learn to do something only to be told it would be easier if the putative instructor just did the job alone will know part of the frustration of liberals in the Arab world. Building a commonwealth is indeed a complex project, but for that very reason, it cannot be bought off the shelf in some ideological supermarket and delivered fully assembled.

It will only be in working with allies like these liberals that we will be able to fully understand the nature of the deeper troubles that spawned the attacks. Judging from what our potential allies are already telling us, in the *Arab Human Development Report* and elsewhere, the lack of investment in education, in scientific research and development, in empowering women has had a corrosive effect on the economies and societies of the region, leaving too many young people, ignorant, frustrated, and understandably furious. There is much the rest of the world, including the United States, could do to rectify those deficits.

To do so, however, requires more than simply directing aid and technical assistance to family-planning projects, investing in local universities and scientific research centers, providing tax credits to technology companies willing to invest in building the information technology infrastructure in the region—although all of that would be desirable. It requires more than simply resisting the temptation to view policy toward the region wholly through the lens of terrorism and counterterrorism—although that is essential. It requires, most important, much greater respect for and fidelity to the liberal values to which we say we adhere, both at home and abroad.

4 International Humanitarian Legal Standards and the Principle of Global Ethics in the War on Terrorism

El Hassan bin Talal

The philosopher Jean-François Revel has said, "The ideologist twists the neck of reality to suit his ideologies, whilst the seeker of truth gives up his ideologies to understand reality." Revel's insight is worth pondering in the midst of the war on terrorism, because terrorism is at once about ideology and reality. Likewise, the place of law and norms in international politics is also a matter of ideology and reality. It is the nexus of the two that should particularly concern us today.

Since September 11, 2001, a quantum leap has occurred in our shared vulnerability and shared consciousness. We inhabit "one world and ten thousand cultures." However, unless the various actors, including the United Nations, nongovernmental organizations, transnational corporations, civil society, and individuals, are given the opportunity to be understood, and unless lateral thinking develops between these many and varied entities, multilateralism will inevitably fall to unilateralism, both in ideology and in reality.

Law is critical to the articulation of an effective multilateralism. According to UN under-secretary-general for legal affairs, Hans Corell, "International law is theoretically about justice and the rule of law but, more immediately, it is about accommodation, not just political accommodation but accommodation of principles and values based upon the interrelationship, or interexistence, of humankind."[1] Here, ideology meets reality in a constructive sense, so that in this context, the United Nations is a necessary institution in world politics, which is, by nature, multilateral. Bulldozing this institution endangers sacrificing universalism at the altar of rogue imperialism.

Law and the War on Terrorism

The world's major faith traditions share the belief that the use of armed force may only be justified in self-defense, on behalf of a grave cause, as an option of last resort, and even then subject to strict limitations. Restarting the dialogue in international law is fundamentally about preserving the universality of the human values and ethical traditions that world religions have long championed and promoted.

In Islam, it is clear that the Qur'an is a pluralistic scripture, affirmative of other traditions as well as its own.[2] It is not only in the "West" that many are asking why it is that the understanding of the Divine is often distorted through the prism of violence.[3] Muslim jurists have historically reacted sharply

---

1. Hans Corell, "Developing the Rule of Law among Nations: A Challenge to the United Nations," The Steinkraus-Cohen International Law Lecture, London, July 7, 2003.

2. Karen Armstrong in *The Guardian,* June 20, 2002.

3. Akbar S. Ahmed, "Islam and the Rest of the World," speech to the Muslim Council in Washington, D.C., 2003.

against groups that were deemed enemies of humankind.[4] Those groups were designated as *muharibs* (literally "fighters") who spread terror in society and were not to be given refuge by anyone at any place. According to Khaled Abou el Fadl, Muslim jurists have historically argued that any Muslim or non-Muslim territory sheltering such a group is hostile territory that may be attacked by legitimate, mainstream Islamic forces. Most important, these doctrines were asserted as religious *imperatives*. Regardless of the desired goals or ideological justifications, the terrorizing of the defenseless was recognized as a moral wrong and an offense against society and God.

The debate within Islamic intellectual circles about the appropriate Islamic response to terrorism has also placed the question of suicide bombings at center stage. Authors such as Sohail Hashmi, for example, have discussed challenges to two fundamental principles of Islamic ethics: the prohibitions against suicide and the deliberate killing of noncombatants.[5] Suicide for any reason has been strongly condemned throughout Islamic history, and its practice is extremely rare in Islamic societies. In the context of war, however, the line between suicide and combat is often extremely fine and easily crossed. Nonetheless, Hashmi contends, the Prophet Muhammad sought to draw a clear line separating martyrdom in battle from suicide: "The Muslim fighter enters battle not with the intention of dying, but with the conviction that if he should die, it is for reasons beyond his control. Martyrdom is the Will of God, not humans."

Others have been even more Islamically unequivocal, stat-

4. See Khaled Abou el Fadl, "Islam: Images, Politics, Paradox," *Middle East Report* 221 (Winter 2001), in *Islam and the Theology of Power* (Los Angeles: UCLA Center for the Study of Religion, 2001).

5. Sohail H. Hashmi, "Not What the Prophet Would Want: How Can Islamic Scholars Sanction Suicidal Tactics?" *Washington Post*, June 9, 2002.

ing that the "religion" of Osama bin Laden has more in common with movements that arise out of a "cultic milieu," or "a parallel religious tradition of disparaged and deviant interpretations and practices that challenge the authority of prevailing religions with rival claims to truth."[6] The latter interpretation of jihad legitimizes violence and terror as a theological imperative—jihadism. Illusions thus come to dominate reality as sloganism takes hold among sections of disenfranchised and disgruntled populations.[7] Amid such an ideational reality, Ziaddun Sardar argues that "a persuasive moral God is replaced by a coercive, political one."

At the political level, the September 11 attacks have been described, among other things, as a violation of Islamic law and ethics. Neither the people killed or injured nor the properties destroyed qualified as legitimate targets in any system of law, especially Islamic law. That position was reinforced by public statements and communiqués, such as the Final Statement of the Emergency Conference of Islamic States' Foreign Ministers in Doha, Qatar, a month after the atrocities.

At a more fundamentally grassroots level, it is difficult to disagree with Muslim commentators, such as Sayyid Rida al-Sadiq: "One of the most painful spectacles for any principled Muslim to behold these days is that of enraged Muslim sentiment being paraded as Islamic 'Jihad.'" Indeed, it is paradoxical that "those who are most fanatical about the forms of the religion end up violating those very forms themselves: suicide and mass murder are alike illegal in any school of Islamic law.

6. Jean E. Rosenfeld, *The Religion of Usamah bin Ladin: Terror as the Hand of God* (Los Angeles: UCLA Center for the Study of Religion, 2002).

7. Khalid S. al-Khater, "Thinking about Arab-American Relations: A New Perspective," *MERIA* 7, no. 2 (June 2003).

A slippery slope leads from religious formalism to sacrilegious fanaticism."[8]

We cannot ignore the internal challenges that give rise to fanaticism. Lack of political freedom in many Muslim countries undercuts Islamic-Western engagement in numerous ways—from the restrictions it places on media and citizen activism to the ways in which it limits the full expression of the diverse views and cultures that exists in Muslim countries. This is one reason that Muslims *in* the West are a key to cultivating meaningful engagement and mutual respect. It also serves as a reminder of the importance of *intra*communal dialogue in Muslim countries.[9]

The relationship between Islam and Western international law has been uniquely affected by the terrorist attacks of September 11 and the subsequent consecutive "liberations" of Afghanistan and Iraq. But Islam is not a geopolitical entity. It is a universal message capable of integration with diverse and very different cultures, including American and European cultures. When we put aside the idea of a "clash of civilizations" and begin to examine religion, we find widespread agreement on principles and humanitarian aims, especially among the three great monotheistic faiths. Bridges of understanding need to be established between Muslim countries and the West, with emphasis on education, media, and young people. There is an urgent need to communicate about America to the Muslim world and for Americans to gain increased understanding of Muslim cultures. This must not to be done in the form of propaganda disguised as educational outreach. It should instead be done positively, honestly, and seriously, at a level

8. Sayyid Rida al-Sadiq, "At War with the Spirit of Islam," *Dialogue* (London) (August 2003).

9. Report of Partners in Humanity Working Meeting, Amman, Jordan, July 26–29, 2003.

fully commensurate with the challenges of the post–September 11 world—a world that has brought to the fore an array of complex issues relating to citizenship, foreign policy, and civil and political rights.[10]

In the aftermath of September 11, the overwhelming majority of Muslim individuals and organizations condemned the attacks unequivocally. Yet, in the minds of many Muslims in the West, a clear distinction was felt between the unacceptability of the act itself and the very genuine grievances it purported to represent. The media, however, and some leaders (notably Silvio Berlusconi of Italy and Margaret Thatcher of the United Kingdom) tended, in some cases, to blur the distinction. For the Muslim community, the immediate fallout from the attacks was dual: On the one hand was the community's explicit condemnation of the attacks. On the other was the fact that this community still faced a kind of public inquisition over its loyalty to the state, which later fed into the rekindling of debates relating to civil liberties. In polarized settings, social solidarity, the cornerstone of citizenship, may be embedded in racial—not civic—networks, affecting the way the public domain is governed.[11] This, one would argue, applies at both the international as well as the domestic level of policy making.

Do we want the world to collapse into a Hobbesian state of nature, which, if one believes humanity to be essentially good, is an unnatural state of affairs? That is the fear if multilateralism fails to hold sway against unilateralism in international law and order. Alongside the strident voices of the hawks in

10. Sayyed Nadeem Kazmi, "Educational Outreach in Muslim States: Implications and Responses," *The Conflict, Security and Development Group Bulletin*, Department for International Development, London (March–April 2002).

11. United Nations Research Institute for Social Development (UNRISD) Conference on Racism and Public Policy, September 3–5, 2001, Durban, South Africa.

Washington, crying for broader strikes against perceived targets in the Middle East, other voices are calling for more measured and culturally sensitive approaches that will provide security for the future—the "soft security" of human dignity, self-worth, and confidence. For instance, a Council on Foreign Relations report concluded that the long-term vision for Iraq, among other things, should "welcome the fullest possible involvement in peacekeeping, reconciliation, and reconstruction efforts by multilateral organisations, such as the United Nations, neighbouring states (especially the Arab world), non-Arab Muslim countries, and other Western partners."[12]

Amid what appears to be an increasingly hegemonic vision for the new world order, it is refreshing and consoling to see many in the United States paying heed to the purposes and principles of the UN Charter, which offers a multilateral approach to the challenges confronting international peace and security, emphasizing development of friendly relations and achievment of international cooperation in a variety of fields. It is during these windows of rational reflection in Washington that one might recall that the United Nations, the international institutions, and the system of alliances and treaty relationships formed in the aftermath of World War II were achieved in large part because of American leadership and engagement.[13] Those institutions and alliances succeeded not because of any specific threat that had emerged but because of a genuine spirit of international cooperation and respect. Isn't it time for all to comply with international laws and norms? A culture of compliance is necessary for our trou-

---

12. Edward P. Djerejian and Frank G. Wisner, *Report of the Independent Working Group*, under the auspices of the Council on Foreign Relations and James Baker III Institute, Washington, D.C., January 23, 2003.

13. Robert T. Grey, Jr., "Warmongering without Representation: Unilateralism Is Not the American Way," *San Francisco Chronicle*, January 15, 2003.

bled world. Any attempt to change the existing laws and norms should come from within the world's cultures, not from without.

American Realities

Today, American leadership appears to operate within a matrix of fear and isolation, resulting in unilateral militarism and cultural disengagement that are reflected in the passing of Resolution 1373 on September 28, 2001, as a direct response to the events of September 11. That resolution, which essentially accepted the American interpretation of terrorism and support for terrorism, was oblivious to the many far-reaching repercussions and unintended consequences of a measure whose ad hoc nature has since been questioned by human rights organizations, bodies, and personalities. One certainly cannot build good international law in a crisis atmosphere. Nowhere are the repercussions of such an international response (multilateral in ideology, unilateral in reality) more apparent than in the Middle East, where American strategic and economic interests have been articulated through President George W. Bush's proposed Middle East Free Trade Area and Middle East Partnership Initiative "to bring the Middle East into an expanding circle of opportunity."[14]

Expanding circles of opportunity in the Middle East is an exercise in futility as long as U.S. strategy in the region continues to operate according to the priorities of oil and security as opposed to humanitarianism. By 2020, the United States is expected to consume an additional 7.4 million barrels of oil per day, reaching approximately 27.5 million barrels per day (about 24 percent of the world's estimated daily consumption of approximately 112 million barrels per day). It is forecast

14. The quote is from President George W. Bush's speech of May 9, 2003.

that with the continued slow decline of U.S. domestic production over this period, the United States will become gradually *more* dependent on imported oil over the next twenty years.[15]

To articulate a positive vision for all, but to ignore one's own responsibilities to bring that vision about, is perhaps what leads some observers, like Javad Zarif, Iran's ambassador to the United Nations, to argue that Washington is "confusing unilateralism with leadership."[16] Zarif's position is that U.S. hegemonic ambition ignores "our common vulnerability to threats which require close cooperation among members of the international community." Some Americans have taken a similar approach. Senator Joseph Biden has aptly warned that foreign policy cannot be conducted at the extremes:

> What we need isn't the death of internationalism or the denial of stark national interest, but a more enlightened nationalism—one that understands the value of institutions but allows us to use military force, without apology or apprehension if we have to, but does not allow us to be so blinded by the overwhelming power of our armed forces that we fail to see the benefit of sharing the risks and the costs with others. We have to understand and be willing to accept that giving a bigger role to the United Nations and NATO means sharing control. The truth is that we missed a tremendous opportunity after 9/11 to lead in a way that actually encouraged others to follow. We missed an opportunity, in the aftermath of our spectacular military victory, to ask those who were not with us in the war to be partners in the peace.[17]

The irony, particularly in the context of the ideology/reality

15. J.A. Russell, "Searching for a Post-Saddam Regional Security Architecture," *MERIA* 7, no. 2 (March 2003).

16. H.E. Javad Zarif, "Indispensable Power: Hegemonic Tendencies in a Globalized World," *Harvard International Review* (Winter 2003).

17. Senator Joseph Biden, "National Dialogue on Iraq + One Year," The Brookings Institution, Washington, D.C., July 31, 2003.

dichotomy, is that while the United States sees itself as supporting freedom from oppression, in the region itself, the United States is, as Soumaya Ghanoushi has put it, "widely regarded by many . . . as a crucial obstacle in [the] struggle for freedom from oppression."[18]

The European Perspective

The European Union has recognized both the link among development, poverty, and conflict and the role of development cooperation in conflict prevention: "Violent conflict causes massive humanitarian suffering, undermines development and human rights and stifles economic growth."[19] Moreover, one might recall the 1999 Hague Appeal for Peace, which is dedicated to "the delegitimization of war, seeking to refocus on a world vision wherein violent conflict is publicly acknowledged as illegitimate, illegal, and fundamentally unjust." To ensure that conflict prevention and peace-building form a central part of development policy, the EU declares that it is important that the issue be further "mainstreamed" within EU policy.

The United States should perhaps follow the EU example in developing and integrating a civilian crisis management capacity in the Middle East. From a peace-building perspective, more attention certainly needs to be given to linking crisis management with longer-term conflict prevention strategies. In the Middle East, in particular, what is needed is a code of conduct, a "partnership for peace," an Eastern Mediterranean Treaty Organization, or perhaps a Middle Eastern

18. Soumaya Ghanoushi, "The Origins of Extremism: Theology or Reality?" *Islam* 21 (London) (December 2001).

19. "Ensuring Progress in the Prevention of Violent Conflict," priorities for the Greek and Italian EU presidencies 2003, April 2003.

version of the Organization for Security and Cooperation in Europe (OSCE).

An articulation of the relevant agenda for any such organization would include the need for a WMD-free zone; a clear definition of terror (both state and nonstate); concrete steps, adequately funded, to redress both manifestations and causes of terror; a humanitarian Marshall Plan (as opposed to a "martial" plan, the likes of which we still see in so many postconflict arenas); transparency guaranteed by government, with a focus on poverty alleviation; education; and interactive citizens' media whereby the people of the region can promote their own dialogue.

If the European Union is dedicated to true multilateralism and appreciates the impact of "soft power" in today's world, perhaps it will lead such a new architectural effort.

Breaking the Political Economy of Despair

As a member of the group of advisers to the UN Dialogue of Civilizations process, I was struck by the aptness of the phrase "the indignities of the 1990s." The aim was, of course, to counterbalance those indignities by creating a paradigmatic shift in our ideas about where we, as humanity, are and how we wish to move forward. Also, as a member of the high-level panel charged by the UN secretary-general to work with the high commissioner for human rights to follow up on the action plan of the 2001 World Conference against Racism, I believe this could be done by following "a humanitarian vision based on an 'ethic of human solidarity,' stressing the centrality of human dignity, respect for diversity and the importance of effective measures of protection for civilians," as emphasized by this panel. "A possible way to achieve this could be through the development of a 'Racial Equality Index' similar to the

'Human Development Index' developed and used by the United Nations Development Programme."

Perhaps thinking globally and acting regionally—which requires a sharing not only of ideas but also of the instruments and tools, including international law, that make such cooperation viable and successful—will help shift not only our entrenched ideological positions but the reality as well. The overemphasis on the military dimension has, in the past, given rise to what may be termed the political economy of despair. My late brother, His Majesty King Hussein, put it this way at Sharm el-Sheikh, Egypt, in 1996:

> The murder and torture of innocent people is not exclusive to one race or nation or to followers of any one religion. It is vital therefore that terrorism be tackled at the international level in a multilateral way, and not in a gung-ho partisan manner. Thus, there is an urgent need to develop a universally acceptable global ethic of human solidarity in which the term "ethics" ought not to be limited to the moral aspect only, but also cover the common sociocultural values that are universal and which have stood the test of time. Implicit within this ethic of human solidarity is the requirement for an overarching matrix of International Humanitarian and Human Rights Law.

The question is, will Washington limit itself to a merely punitive agenda to treat only the symptoms of crisis in the Muslim world? In the international coalition at this time, Muslim countries have to take the initiative and attempt to provide a solution rather than just follow America or Britain. The Organization of the Islamic Conference condemned the September 11 attacks but linked the fight against terrorism with the Palestinian situation. One cannot deny the centrality of Palestine to the wider question, but the Muslim world needs to build a coalition among its own states that will twist the neck of current reality by moving toward the creation of integrated strategies that will delegitimize the terrorists, drain the proverbial swamp, *and* deal with its root causes. As seekers of truth, we owe future generations the legacy of a new reality based on global commons.

5 | Ending Support for Terrorism in the Muslim World

Michele Durocher Dunne

On September 11, 2001, I was finishing lunch in Cairo with an Egyptian friend when I received a call on my mobile phone with shocking news. As I relayed the news to Mohammed bit by bit, we both rose from our seats and fled—I to the U.S. embassy (where I was a political officer), and he to an office of the Egyptian presidency (where he was an adviser). After a few initial days of understandable security panic, the embassy opened a book of condolences. Soon Egyptians from many walks of life—diplomats and business tycoons, yes, but also entire classes of schoolchildren—lined up for days to sign that book, many of them weeping and bearing flowers.

At the same time, however, the international media conveyed images of Egyptians and other Arabs expressing joy, or at least grim satisfaction, at the attacks. Over the ensuing months, many Egyptians who professed to be friends to the United States said to me, in effect, "I'm sorry this happened, but you had it coming."

With this mixed picture as background, let us pose two questions: What is the problem the United States faces in the Muslim world? And what should we do about it?

Regarding what to do, as a start, I posit that the U.S. government, with all the many tools and vast power at its disposal, cannot directly change the thinking or behavior of Muslims who support the use of terrorism. Nor can the U.S. government directly alter the policies of Middle Eastern governments that acquiesce to terrorism, play double games with terrorists, or oppress their people in ways that feed terrorism. And clearly, the U.S. government cannot use, ought not use, and in any case has no intention of using military force against every country in the Middle East whose counterterrorism policies we find less than perfect.

It is equally important to know, however, what the U.S. government *can* do. It can put the tremendous power and influence it possesses to work in combating both the phenomenon of terrorism itself and the problems that give rise to support for terrorism among Muslims. To do this, however, the U.S. government would need to change the way it deals with governments of Arab and other Muslim countries. Doing so would require an integrated policy approach, not just military and law-enforcement efforts dressed up with public diplomacy.

To say any more of such an approach, however, requires us to first return to the problem.

What the Problem Is ... and Is Not

In addition to the phenomenon of terrorist acts themselves— which has been the focus of intensive military, diplomatic, and law-enforcement efforts since September 2001—there is the nagging issue of why many (though by no means all) Muslims in various parts of the world expressed the opinion after September 11 that the attacks were justified or at least understandable. American observers have suggested a number of explanations: that active or passive support for the use of terrorism springs from something endemic to Islam or to Arab culture; that such support springs from the perceived threat that American culture and globalization pose to Islam; that such support is a response to oppression by local rulers; that such support reflects strong objections to U.S. policies in the Middle East.

The fact that those who carried out the attacks of September 11 (and other Muslims who saw those attacks as justified in some way) came originally from countries where they were oppressed politically and otherwise, and that they nursed deep grievances against U.S. policies, is difficult to deny. Regarding the Arab countries in particular, I have often been struck by the difficulty of disentangling the various sources of grievance toward the United States. It is as if there were a deep well of resentment with various contributing streams—American policy regarding Israel and Palestine; the U.S. military presence on the Arabian peninsula and in the Persian Gulf; U.S. support for governments that oppress politically and that are inept or worse economically; and the resulting exclusion of many Arabs from the benefits of globalization, with which, of course, the United States is closely identified.

Anger toward the United States due to its support for Israel, which despite the many years of U.S. efforts for peace often redounds to the disadvantage of Palestinians, is an important factor, but by no means is it the only one. And it is a factor with symbolic as well as actual impact; the Palestinian issue feeds a feeling among many Arabs—and apparently many non-Arab Muslims as well—of humiliation by association.

Similarly, the presence of U.S. military forces in Saudi Arabia (greatly reduced in the summer of 2003) and elsewhere in the region creates another source of humiliation for Muslims, who see it as demonstrating that they are unable to deal with their most basic problems, even the protection of their own sacred places. Needless to say, U.S. military action to remove Saddam Hussein's regime and the resulting occupation of Iraq merely point out one more glaring problem that Arabs have been unable to take care of themselves.

In addition to the more obvious problems of Palestine and Iraq, it is many Arabs' sense of helplessness in changing their own very difficult domestic political and economic conditions that fuels their anger at the United States. The United States is almost universally held responsible, whether fairly or not, for supporting the governments that perpetuate those terrible conditions. It is on this matter that I will focus in describing what the problem is and how to address it.

Arguably, grievances, however deeply felt, do not fully explain why horrific violence against innocent people is viewed as a legitimate response. But bitter feelings of humiliation and helplessness, spiked with the Islamic extremists' call to reject and attack the new global order authored by the United States, make a powerful brew. One way to capture this dynamic is through an economic metaphor: there is a desperate demand for solutions to desperate problems in the Arab world, and a well-funded supply of Islamic extremist ideas and groups rise to meet that demand.

The supply side of the question—namely, the funding and political support of Islamic extremist ideas and groups exported from the Arabian Peninsula to many other Arab and Muslim countries — is undoubtedly a serious problem. Cutting off funds and other forms of support to those who either commit terrorist attacks or justify them through religious or political teachings is indispensable. It must be a top priority within the context of an overall strategy.

Dealing with the supply side alone, however, is not enough, because extremists in many countries have deep roots and can easily replace recruits who are captured or killed. The demand side is just as important. In other words, if Saudi Arabia (and Iran, for that matter) were to disappear from the face of the earth tomorrow, Islamic extremists would survive in many other countries, unaided from the outside, because miserable local conditions have created a demand (and a large pool of recruits) for the radical solutions the extremists feign to supply.

In thinking about how the United States should approach the conditions that generate a demand or support for terrorism, I start from the premise that American influence and resources in the Arab world have not been, are not now, and cannot be neutral. To quote Bob Dylan, "We're gonna have to serve somebody," and a serious rethinking of whom in the Arab world our policies and assistance programs are serving is long overdue.

There are two realities that we need to acknowledge before we can get anywhere. First, until recently, U.S. priorities in the region have been so narrowly drawn—security of oil supplies; guaranteed military access; a sometimes cautious, sometimes energetic pursuit of Israeli-Palestinian peace—as to cause the United States to bolster regimes whose domestic policies are economic and political disasters. Although not necessarily the intent of the U.S. government, it remains the case that Arab domestic issues were ignored for too many years. The Bush administration deserves credit for being the first to see things differently, and the president's National Endowment for Democracy speech of November 6, 2003, is by far the most dramatic presidential statement on this issue in more than half a century. But it remains unclear how seriously and skillfully the issue will be addressed.

Second, the State Department has devoted far too little attention to managing diplomatic relationships in the Arab world, in many cases leaving that job to the Defense Department. One need only contrast the record of frequent, routinely scheduled travel by senior Defense Department officials to Egypt, Saudi Arabia, Jordan, and other Arab countries in recent years (long before September 11 and the war in Iraq) with the infrequent trips of senior State Department officials. The huge imbalance of resources that the two departments have in hand, plus the absence of any State Department equivalent to the military commanders in chief who can operate on a regional basis, only compounds the implications of the lack of high-level State Department leadership.

One consequence of all this was that as long as our basic needs, narrowly defined, were being assured, little effort was devoted to all the other aspects of our relationships with these countries. We did not bother much to manage impressions, refute untruths, or pay close attention to political, economic, and social life inside these countries.

To sum up then, what is the problem? The problem, we now realize, is that what goes on inside Middle Eastern countries has important security consequences for us. Unfortunately, our ability to affect those goings-on has been compromised by the legacy of our attending exclusively to more traditional security problems—namely, those of the Cold War. What is not the problem? The problem is not proving whether everything the Arabs say about the United States and U.S. policy is true. We cannot escape from the fact that the conditions under which Arabs and many other Muslims live lead them to believe it is all true.

What to Do . . . and Not to Do

If the United States must now begin to concern itself with domestic conditions in Arab countries with which it has important relationships (and in some cases significant assistance programs), how should it do so?

American influence, though far from neutral, is also generally indirect. With few exceptions, we cannot directly change conditions in other countries, and in any case, we would not be willing to commit the resources required even to make a serious attempt. It is instructive to remember what any twelve-step program tells its participants: you cannot change another person or his or her behavior directly. What the United States *can* do is change its own behavior toward the governments in question, which in turn would change dynamics between the United States and actors (whether governments or not) in those countries, and which, in turn, may cause those actors to change their behavior.

It hardly wants emphasis that this process is unpredictable and not completely controllable. But it has the virtue of being based in reality and has a reasonable chance of success. Self-delusion or arguing about our ability to change things directly does not.

A policy review must also start from the premise that something is seriously amiss regarding any country where we have a significant relationship, but where there is nonetheless significant support for anti-U.S. terrorism. We need to understand which forces our current relationships are serving and how we would have to change those relationships so that they serve those inside and outside governments whose interests accord with ours and who will give their people a stake in a viable system: forces for liberal, market economies; for the rule of law and respect for women's rights; for accountable, participatory political systems; for religious toleration and nonviolence. Nothing less will suit—not these days.

Any such strategy must involve all the tools at the U.S. government's disposal: diplomatic engagement, military relationships, assistance programs, public diplomacy, and engagement with American private enterprise and nongovernmental organizations. Public diplomacy efforts—glossy magazines for Arab youth, satellite television to compete with al-Jazeera, pop radio programs like Radio Sawa and Radio Farda, campaigns to show religious tolerance and diversity in the United States—are positive in their own way. But they have impact only if accompanied by a responsible reorientation of our policies and assistance programs. Arabs, Iranians, Pakistanis, and others are not stupid people; they will not buy rhetoric without a corresponding reality for very long.

Similarly, assistance programs to promote political and economic reform and to improve education or free media, for example, will fall flat or backfire unless they are part of an overall strategy of engagement with governments. Simply put, how seriously will any Arab leader take our assistance or public diplomacy programs to promote reform and moderation when those subjects are never on the agenda of high-level conversations?

For policy purposes, we need a country-by-country diagnosis of the nature of the problem—specifically, why people in Saudi Arabia or Egypt or Pakistan or Indonesia would support or sympathize with those who commit or advocate terrorism against Americans. The reasons need not be, and probably are not, the same in every case. Next, we need to look with fresh eyes at what the United States can do—and what the United States should urge the governments in question to do—to address the problems and grievances that have led to this sad state of affairs.

Following the diagnosis and a cold-eyed examination of our current relations with what involves twenty-two Arab countries and at least that many more majority-Muslim countries, the U.S. government should formulate policy to begin the long, messy, and uncertain process of using our influence to push things in the right direction. No doubt, we will need to work with other major donors, including international financial institutions, to multiply our efforts.

All of this will be difficult and will involve painstaking work. The furthest the Bush administration has gone in addressing underlying support for terrorism in the Arab world has been through the Middle East Partnership Initiative (MEPI), announced by Secretary of State Powell in December 2002. The initiative seeks to use existing and new economic assistance to Middle East countries to promote economic, political, and educational reform and the empowerment of women. Although the initiative is undoubtedly positive and deserves support, it is not, or not yet, a comprehensive strategy. It is still divorced from U.S. military assistance, for example, and has little connection to public diplomacy efforts. Moreover, there is no parallel initiative for Muslims outside the Middle East in such important countries as Indonesia, Pakistan, or Nigeria.

So what to do? We need to take the domestic political, economic, and social dynamics of Arab and Muslim countries seriously, and we need to rebalance our overall policy objectives to reflect that reality. What not to do? We do not have to ruin existing relationships with the Saudi, Egyptian, and other Arab governments, or undermine Israeli security, or abandon our interests in the traditional objectives of oil, peace, and strategic access. The task is hard enough as it is without painting it as both impossible and ridiculous. What is needed is a filling out and maturation of our relationships with governments and peoples of the region to show that we believe domestic reform is badly needed in many countries, for their good and for ours.

Getting Organized

The Middle East Partnership Initiative offers a window on how the organization of the U.S. government affects its ability to deal with the Muslim world. Strict division of bureaucratic responsibilities along regional lines in the Departments of State and Defense discourages productive thinking about problems that cross regions. Bureaucrats in regional bureaus consider it not only a prerogative but also a duty to combat any transregional priority that might cut into their freedom to make decisions about policies and money within their narrow and short-term perspectives. (Readers who have not worked in the U.S. government might find this statement cynical; those who have are liable to find it a gross understatement.)

That is why there should be a designated high-level official, for example a special assistant to the president, to oversee the development and implementation of policy strategies on using our influence to help end support for terrorism in the Muslim world. The special assistant would coordinate with those working the supply side of the problem (intelligence and law-enforcement efforts to stop terrorist acts, as well as diplomacy to end funding and other forms of support to extremist Islamists), and those working the demand side (diplomatic assistance and public diplomacy efforts to address conditions that generate support for terrorism) to ensure that efforts are coherent and mutually reinforcing. The existing bureaucracy is simply incapable of changing course without strong leadership, and it will tend to cut initiatives (such as MEPI) down to a size that fits into the old scheme of priorities.

The reality is that if there is no one accountable for doing a difficult job in government, that job will not get done. Is it possible that, after the thousands of lives lost and billions of dollars spent on combating terrorism through military action and law enforcement, the U.S. government will fail to effectively combat the underlying sources of support for terrorism because it was simply too much trouble to ask the bureaucracy to operate differently? Yes, it is possible.

Country
Portraits

6 Islam, Modernity, and Public Diplomacy in the Arab World: A Moroccan Snapshot

Dale F. Eickelman

Prior to the coalition invasion in Iraq, one of the hottest topics of intellectual debate in the Arab world, as well as on al-Jazeera satellite television, was "Islam and modernity" (*al-Islam wa al-hadatha*). Discussions of religion and modernity framed even the widely discussed 2002 Arab development report. The fact that such a document is accessible in several languages via the Internet throughout the Arab world and elsewhere also shows the rapidly changing ground rules for public discussion and debate.[1]

Islam and Islam's relation to modern society are central topics in present-day debate and discourse. What is not thoroughly modern and up to date—in the Middle East, Europe, and the United States—are understandings of the role that

1. See Yves Gonzalez-Quijano, "The Birth of a Media Ecosystem: Lebanon in the Internet Age," in *New Media in the Muslim World: The Emerging Public Sphere*, ed. Dale F. Eickelman and Jon W. Anderson (Bloomington: Indiana University Press, 2003), 61–79.

religion plays in contemporary social life. Ironically, the secular bias of Western modernization theory has deflected attention away from the pervasive role of religious practices and values in contemporary societies, particularly in the Muslim-majority world.

Modernization Theory and Religion

In the early 1960s, a leading American public intellectual saw the Muslim world as facing an unpalatable choice: either "neo-Islamic totalitarianism" intent on "resurrecting the past" or a "reformist Islam" that would open "the sluice gates and [be] swamped by the deluge."[2] Another suggested that Middle Eastern societies faced the stark choice of "Mecca or mechanization."[3] At the least, such views suggested an intensely negative assessment of the possibilities of indigenous evolution in Muslim societies.

Common to all variants of modernization theory is the assumption of a declining role for religion, except as a private matter. To move toward modernity, political leaders must displace the authority of religious leaders and devalue the importance of traditional religious institutions. Modernity is seen as an "enlargement of human freedoms" and an "enhancement of the range of choices" as people begin to "take charge" of themselves.[4] In this view, religion can retain its influence only by conforming to the norms of "rationality" and relativism, accepting secularization, and becoming subordinate to science, economic concerns, and the state.

2. Manfred Halpern, *The Politics of Social Change in the Middle East and North Africa* (Princeton, N.J.: Princeton University Press, 1963), 129.

3. Daniel Lerner, *The Passing of Traditional Society: Modernizing the Middle East* (New York: Free Press, 1964 [1958]), 405.

4. T. N. Madan, "Secularism in Its Place," *Journal of Asian Studies* 6 (1987): 747–59.

Recent history offers formidable challenges to Western modernization theory. Of all third world countries, Iran had undergone enormous state-driven modernization prior to 1978–79. Nonetheless, the state's greatest challenge emanated from the growing urban middle classes, those who had benefited the most from modernization. Revolution, not political stability, was the result. Moreover, religious sentiment and leadership, not the secular intelligentsia, gave coherence and force to the revolution.

Modernization theory also deflected attention away from other politically influential religious movements in the 1970s, such as the rise of Solidarity in Poland, liberation theology throughout Latin America, and protestant fundamentalism as a force in American politics. In the words of philosopher Richard Rorty, religion usually functions as a "conversation-stopper" outside of circles of believers.[5] That's why Western modernization experts viewed secular nationalisms, including the rise of the Ba'ath party in Syria and Iraq, as forces for modernization and development.

The Return of Religion

Although it is easy to be critical of Samuel Huntington's "clash" argument because of its reliance on superseded ideas of culture, he was one of the first political scientists to spur colleagues and policy makers to reemphasize the roles of culture and tradition in political and international relations.[6]

---

5. Cited in John Keane, "The Limits of Secularism," *Times Literary Supplement* (January 9, 1999), 12.

6. Samuel Huntington, "The Clash of Civilizations?" *Foreign Affairs* 72, no. 3 (Summer 1993): 22–49. For comments on Huntington's argument as it applies specifically to the Muslim world, see Dale F. Eickelman, "Muslim Politics: The Prospects for Democracy in North Africa and the Middle East," in *Islam,*

Decades before Huntington's argument, sociologist and public intellectual Edward Shils vigorously argued that traditions are not merely unquestioned residues from earlier eras; instead, they are actively maintained clusters of cultural concepts, shared understandings, and practices that make political and social life possible.[7] These pervasive cultural understandings coexist with and shape the experience of modernity. In this sense, ethnicity, caste, and clientelism can be as distinctly modern as the idea of individual choice.

Politics, like religion, is a struggle over people's imaginations, a competition and contest over the meanings of symbols. This means that politics encompasses tradition, not only in the form of practices and shared understandings but also in the interpretation of symbols and the control of institutions, formal and informal, that produce and sustain those symbols. Politics also involves cooperation in and contest over symbolic production and control of the institutions, formal and informal, that serve as the symbolic arbiters of society.

The role of symbolic politics in general, or of "Muslim politics" in the sense of a field for debate as opposed to a bloc of uniform belief and practice, could be seen as less exceptional if the European experience with secularism were kept in mind. Religious discourse was a basic precondition for the rise of the early modern public sphere in Europe.[8] Indeed, contemporary defenders of secularism often exaggerate the durability and open-mindedness of thoroughly secular institutions, be they in the United States, Turkey, or India. In the context

---

Democracy, and the State in North Africa, ed. John Entelis, 35–38 (Bloomington: Indiana University Press, 1997).

7. Edward Shils, *The Intellectuals and the Powers* (Chicago: University of Chicago Press, 1972), 17.

8. Dominique Colas, *Civil Society and Fanaticism: Conjoined Histories,* trans. Amy Jacobs (Stanford: Stanford University Press, 1997).

of the Muslim-majority Middle East, the militant secularism of some governing elites—the Turkish officer corps, for example—has been associated until recently with authoritarianism and intolerance more than with "enlightenment" values.

Because the Muslim-majority world remains feared by those who regard it as the last outpost of the antimodern, the role of religious intellectuals in contributing to an emerging public sphere is often overlooked. This public sphere is rapidly expanding because of the growth of higher education, the increasing ease of travel, and the proliferation of media and means of communication. Both mass education and mass communication, particularly the proliferation of media, profoundly influence how people think about the language of religious and political authority throughout the Muslim world. It is only a minor paradox that a strong indication of modernity is the way in which a decentralized al Qaeda has succeeded in organization and practice in the face of determined efforts to eradicate it.

Terrorism's Thoroughly Modern Face

Terrorism in the name of Islam also has a thoroughly modern face. Osama bin Laden no longer makes many videos, but when he did, his rehearsed message and presentation of self was as thoroughly modern as that of French-educated Pol Pot. Bin Laden may have tried to reinvent a traditional Islamic warrior "look," but his sense of the past is an invented one. The language and content of his videotaped appeals, such as a recruitment video that appeared in late spring of 2001, were even more contemporary than his camouflage jacket, Kalashnikov rifle, and Timex watch. The CNN-like video, complete with "zippers"—running text beneath the images—was as fast-paced as a U.S. Army recruitment video or a U.S. presidential campaign ad.

Indeed, bin Laden is thoroughly imbued with the values of the modern world, even if only to reject them. He studied English at a private school and used English for his civil engineering courses. His many business enterprises flourished under highly adverse conditions. He sustained flexible, multinational organizations in the face of enemies—moving cash, people, and armaments undetected across frontiers.

Unlike most of his colleagues, bin Laden has been a highly visible poster child for transnational religious terrorism. Underestimating the intelligence, commitment, and tenacity of international terrorists would be an error as tragic as assuming that they are on the run. The best candidates for terrorist activities, like candidates for "martyrdom" operations, appear not to be maladjusted, undereducated, suicidal misfits; rather, they are intelligent, committed, motivated individuals willing to sacrifice material and emotional comforts because they regard their religion as their most important personal value.[9] The spring 2001 al Qaeda recruitment video appeals to those wishing to devote themselves to a higher cause, and organized, experienced cadres appear able to recruit those most capable of advancing the cause.

In the past few years, to speak about "public Islam" and the "common good" (al-maslaha al-'amma)—a Qur'anically sanctioned term that has more resonance than calls to civil society and that is used for this purpose by many of those who support civil society—requires tenacity and courage. Colombia may still lead the world in the number of deaths directly attributable to terrorism, but the events of September 11, the

9. For a summary of studies on would-be martyrs and attitudes toward them, see Scott Atran, "Who Wants to Be a Martyr?" *New York Times*, May 5, 2003.

October 2002 bombings in Bali, the May 2003 "kamikaze" attacks in Saudi Arabia and Morocco, the November attacks in Riyadh and Istanbul, and the continued bombings and violence elsewhere, including Jerusalem and Baghdad, test the limits of civility and tolerance. One place to begin looking for changing attitudes is the so-called Arab "street."

The New Arab "Street" in Morocco

The Arab "street"—a term that is rapidly disappearing from Washington shorthand—has rapidly evolved in the past two decades from the shapeless and manipulated image that the term once evoked in the West. Throughout the Arab world, Iran, and Turkey, there is a more concrete awareness than in the past of the benefits and characteristics of more open societies. From March 20, 2003, a day after the first British and U.S. bombs fell on selected targets in Baghdad, until early June of that year, I was "embedded" in the old *madina* of Fez, twelve minutes by fast walk from the nearest drivable road. Complete with donkeys, mules, pushcarts, CD and cassette shops selling the latest pirated pop music, and satellite TVs in coffee shops, Fez's *madina* must qualify as the quintessential Arab "street."

Many of my neighbors lived at the economic edge, buying minuscule amounts of cooking oil and supplies meal by meal and often on credit because of meager incomes. Having been away from Fez for eight years, I was surprised by the prevalence of satellite television or access to it in coffee shops. During the first weeks of the Iraqi invasion, almost everyone's last choice for news was Morocco's state-run television, watched only for the "official" story. Qatar's al-Jazeera satellite TV was usually the channel of choice, although competing Arabic satellite news channels, especially al-'Arabiya, were also closely watched. One did not have to be wealthy to watch satellite TV. Few Fassis read newspapers for understanding the latest events—only 1 percent of Moroccans regularly do. In contrast, about 4 percent of Algerians regularly read newspapers in spite of Algeria's much lower rate of literacy.[10]

After the fall of Saddam's regime—announced April 10 in *Asharq al-Awsat* (London), the premier international Arabic language newspaper; repeated endlessly on most Arab satellite channels; and grudgingly conceded by Morocco's partisan local press—discussion along my particular Arab "street" was uncannily like discussions in the Western press: What happens next? Will America (Britain was scarcely mentioned) bring a better government? What will be the Turkish reaction, especially if Iraq's Kurds are given a voice in government?

Although the term *democracy* (*al-dimuqratiya*) was used only by the educated, many people were aware of restrictions placed on their genuine political participation. Freedom of the press and relief from government manipulation of the electoral political process were themes understood by many more. Discussions of politics and the implications of the "regime change" in Iraq were more animated in private homes than on the Arab "street."

In 2003, the perpetrators of the May 16 bombings in Casablanca carefully timed them as a media event. Moroccans were finishing a week of celebrations for the naming ceremony for the monarch's first child, Hassan III. The evening news on state television was still showing images of celebrations throughout the country and the monarch's visits to major religious shrines in Fez and Meknes. In Marrakech, on the night of May 15, I witnessed dancing in the streets (young

---

10. Oumama Draoui, "*Le livre dans un piteux état*," *Le Journal hebdomadaire* (Casablanca), (May 3–9, 2003): 28.

men only, of course, as is locally "proper") and heard a band playing the then popular Arabic song, "Give Me a Visa, Give Me a Passport." The televised pageantry the next evening was splendid and the television announcers breathless in proclaiming the people's joy and unity with the 'Alawi dynasty and the king's designated successor, the infant "deputy of the era" (*wali al-'ahd*). The coordinated bomb attacks in the center of Casablanca were aimed at Jewish and foreign targets, including the Jewish cemetery next to the old *madina*, a Spanish restaurant, and a hotel often used by tourists from Israel and in which a Moroccan-American seminar on counterterrorism had just concluded. These attacks quickly displaced news of the royal birth.

The May 17 evening television news showed the devastation, including photographs of the mainly Moroccan victims and their relatives. The king visited the scenes of carnage and comforted the survivors; television showed all. The palace spokesperson declared that the investigation would be "transparent," punishment of the perpetrators would be "without mercy," and Morocco's steps toward "democracy" would not be derailed—the latter of which was a reference to local elections postponed from April to September 2003 because of concerns of growing Islamist influence.

The public face of response was horror and shock. The private face is harder to read. Because the monarch spoke out, few people offered contrary opinions in public. After a summer 1994 terrorist bombing in Marrakech's main square, the Djema'a el-Fina, the national manhunt quickly tracked down the perpetrators and had widespread popular support. As one Islamic activist explained to me at the time, this was a national issue, not a political one, and people volunteered leads to the police throughout Morocco.

A similar outcome to the 2003 bombings will offer a measure of the current balance of political forces. Although Moroccans spoke less about the Casablanca bombings than they did about the invasion of Iraq in late March and early April 2003, the level of public awareness and concern was high. A few days after the Casablanca bombings, state television was filled with images of projects to relieve the desperate poverty of Morocco's shantytowns. The Ministry of Education announced that illiteracy rates will be reduced in the next few years, and the Ministry of Pious Endowments and Religious Affairs announced plans to remove extremist preachers from mosques. Many Moroccans, including journalists with some of the small circulation weekly reviews, have rediscovered the "forgotten" inhabitants, such as the squalid Sidi Moumen shantytown on the outskirts of Casablanca, home to most of Casablanca's May 16 "kamikaze" bombers. Yet most Moroccans remain skeptical about how long or how deep this "rediscovery" of Morocco's poor and disadvantaged will persist.

The Japanese term *kamikaze*, the preferred term used by Moroccan government spokespeople in the wake of the Casablanca bombings, was an interesting choice because it avoided the direct invocation of a religious term, such as the Arabic *shahid* ("martyr") or its direct denial as *intihari* ("suicide"). *Kamikaze* carries less contextual baggage, and thus becomes the first Japanese term to enter Moroccan colloquial usage and Arabic usage in general. It also possibly indicates the ambivalence of state spokespeople in public about choosing Arabic terms that would have unequivocally denied religious legitimacy to all those who would use such tactics in support of causes elsewhere. The good news is that the invocation of a Japanese term at least occasioned public, although not broadcast, discussion and debate. One wonders, however, how long it will be before people start using the term *Islamikaze*.

Discovering Open Societies and Making Them Work

The substantial growth in mass education over the past three decades, the proliferation and accessibility of new media and communications, and the increasing ease of travel make it impossible for state and religious authorities to monopolize the tools of literature and culture. The ideas, images, and practices of alternative social and political worlds have become a daily occurrence. They enter domestic space through satellite and cable television, and the alternate realities are better understood than in the past. Rapidly rising literacy levels and familiarity with an educated Arabic formerly restricted to an elite facilitate this better comprehension. They also rehearse viewers to respond to those in authority in the common Arabic of the classroom and the media.

Ideas of just rule, religious or otherwise, are not fixed, even if some radicals claim otherwise. Such notions are debated, argued, often fought about, and re-formed in practice. Such debates are occurring throughout the region. A needed first step is to recognize the contours, obstacles, and false starts, both internal to the region's different countries and external, to making governance less arbitrary and authoritarian.

In April 2003, a Moroccan journalist, commenting on the shortcomings of Morocco's September 2002 elections and their relevance to the September 2003 local elections, wrote, "I am no longer interested in transparency as an end in itself, but rather as an instrument of political negotiation to brandish several months prior to [our] local elections." He concluded, "Communication does not necessarily mean credibility."[11] Perhaps not. However, the ability to communicate in a com-

---

11. Driss Ksikes, "*Un Hold-up avorté?*" *Tel Quel* 72 (April 5–11, 2003): 28–37.

mon language, confront authority in it, compare multiple sources of information on other people's experiences with similar issues elsewhere, and obtain reliable information and share it rapidly—abilities held until recently only by state authorities and a political elite—have dramatically changed shared understandings of religion and politics throughout the Arab Middle East. They have also altered the prospects for open societies and democracy.

The government's response to the November terrorist attacks is being carefully watched by all Moroccans, and efforts to characterize Islamists in general as "Stalinist fascists" or "intellectual fascists" may suffer severe backlash, especially in cities such as Casablanca, Tangier, Fez, Meknes, Rabat, and Marrakech, as well as in the universities, where Islamist thought and practice—although not terrorism—are gaining ground faster than the government and many others care to admit.

Such challenges are not regional alone, and foreign powers that act in the region to encourage more open societies must now match deeds with words. Successes, like shortcomings, will now become known in real time. Modernity offers opportunities as well as challenges. If U.S. military strength and efficacy is now matched by a persuasive and effective public diplomacy that works, encouraging open societies and making progress in resolving even the Israeli-Palestinian dispute, then we will have the most powerful means imaginable to turn the Arab "street" into a forum in which vast numbers of people, not just a political and economic elite, will have a say.

Of course, many of these voices will seek ideas of just rule in religion. We may find this use of religion in the public square unfamiliar, but, as in Turkey and possibly in postwar Iraq, the religiously committed can learn to become moderates and to work toward achieving open societies. Although achieving this goal will be more demanding than was regime change in Iraq, it is an opportunity that can, and must, be seized.

7 | The Challenges of Euro-Islam

Olivier Roy

Even if Islam-related terrorist attacks in Europe never achieve the level of those perpetrated in the United States or Indonesia, western Europe has played a major role as a base for planning and organization for al Qaeda's cells: the World Trade Center (WTC) attack was planned by the Hamburg cell of al Qaeda; Ahmed Ressam was linked with a French radical network; Richard Reid was recruited in a British jail; and Zacharias Moussaoui found his calling in a London mosque.

Moreover, al Qaeda is not the only radical Islamic group active in western Europe. Other networks (like Kelkal in 1995 and the Roubaix group in 1996) have acted independently, mostly sharing ideas and recruiting along patterns similar to those of al Qaeda. Similarly, new independent groups could arise in the future. The issue of radicalization and violence thus goes beyond the present problem posed by al Qaeda and could continue or increase even if al Qaeda itself is destroyed.

This is, roughly speaking, the scope of the challenge of Euro-Islam.

Who Are the Terrorists?

Islamic radicals in western Europe fall roughly into three categories: foreign residents, second-generation immigrants (most often native-born), and converts.

The first category is that of young Middle Easterners who come to Europe as students, mostly in modern disciplines, who speak Arabic, and who are from middle-class backgrounds. The WTC pilots are an excellent example of this first category, who often become born-again Muslims only after coming to Europe and before joining a radical group.

The second category is made up of second-generation European Muslims, some educated but many more school dropouts, who usually come from rather destitute neighborhoods. They speak European languages as their first language and often are European citizens.

The third category, the smallest in number but not necessarily in significance, is made up of converts, many of whom became Muslim while spending time in jail.

Members of all three categories follow the same general trajectory of radicalization, the key to which is that they break ties with their milieu of origin. They almost invariably become born-again Muslims (or converts) by joining a mosque known to host radical imams, and soon after that (in the span of less than a year), they turn politically radical and go (or try to go) to fight a jihad abroad. Before September 11, that meant going to Afghanistan. Since May 2003, it may mean going to Iraq.[1]

1. Hard evidence and data remain elusive; see Desmond Butler and Don Van Natta, Jr., "Trail of Anti-U.S. Fighters Said to Cross Europe to Iraq," *New York Times*, December 6, 2003.

It is noteworthy that almost *none* of these radicals have gone to their country of origin or of their families' origin to wage jihad. And they have usually gone to the "peripheral" jihad—to Bosnia, Chechnya, Afghanistan, Kashmir, or New York—rather than to the Middle East. (Two Pak-Britons did perpetrate a terrorist attack in Tel Aviv in spring 2003, but this is, so far, the only exception to the rule.)

In addition, almost all of these terrorists broke completely with their families only after entering their process of radicalization. Having done so, they usually became urban nomads of sorts, often changing places and even countries. Thus, these terrorists are largely supranational and socially atomized. They also tend to have a Westernized trajectory in studies (urban planning, computer science), in languages (all are fluent in Western languages), and in matrimonial affairs (often marrying or dating European women).

Such a Western profile is not only a function of their sociological situation, it is also a condition of success: they live in total immersion in a Western society. The strength and the weakness of Islamic radicals in western Europe is precisely their lack of rooting among the European Muslim population. The strengths are that they can hardly be spotted by the police before going into action or be traced by police penetration of the local Muslim population. It is also difficult to penetrate their networks because they are cut off from the outside world and are highly mobile. But the weakness is that they have problems of recruitment and logistics because they do not relate well to ordinary "civilian" fellow Muslims.

Reasons for Radicalization

There is no clear-cut sociological profile of the Islamic radicals beyond that sketched out above. There is nothing exact or precise to link them to a given socioeconomic situation. More precisely, the reasons that may push them toward violence are not specific enough and include such characteristics shared by a larger population that deals with similar situations in very different ways. Explanations based on poverty, exclusion, racism, acculturation, and so forth may contain kernels of truth, but they are not specific enough to be of much practical help in stopping terrorists from acting.

For example, there is clearly a generational dimension at work here. Islamic radicalism is a youth movement. Frustration is obviously a key element in their radicalization, but it seems to have more to do with a particular psychological dimension than with a social or economic one. A common factor among known radicals is a concern for self-image and a desire to reconstruct the self through action. In this sense, young radicals are more in search of an opportunity for spectacular action where they will be personally and directly involved than with the long-term, patient building of a political organization that could extend the social and political base of their networks. They are more present-oriented activists than future-oriented constructivists. They are thus far different from the Comintern agents of the 1920s and 1930s.

This narcissist dimension explains both the commitment to suicide actions and the difficulty such people have in working underground without the perspective and prospect of action. Without terrorism, they do not exist. This commitment to immediate or midterm action, as opposed to long-term political action, is probably the greatest weakness of radical Islamism in Europe, but it also makes them very hard to catch and stop.

But clearly, only a small fraction of alienated Muslim youth evinces these characteristics. Very few become terrorists. There is no obvious or practical way to tell one trajectory from others because, as noted above, it is less sociological than psychological.

Another significant pattern in Euro-Islamist radicalization is the blending of Islamic wording and phraseology with a typically Western anti-imperialism and third-worldist radicalism. For the most part, Euro-Islamist targets are the same ones that the Western ultra-Leftist movements of the 1970s identified. Islamists, however, seek mass terrorism, and they do not target political or business personalities, as the European ultra-Left used to do. Nevertheless, the paradigm of ultra-Leftist terrorism from the 1970s might provide a bridge in future to non-Islamic radicals, perhaps even to some in the so-called antiglobalization movement.

But again, such ideologies are believed by many Islamic residents in western Europe, and only a few such ideologues become terrorists. So, we can array several perhaps necessary conditions for identifying an Islamist terrorist in Europe, but we cannot specify what the sufficient conditions are.

Threats and Perspectives

Since September 11 and the anti-Taliban campaign in Afghanistan, Islamist terrorists have been faced with two new problems that have immediate consequences for their ability to act in or from western Europe: organizational problems and political problems.

No longer is there easy sanctuary for Islamist radicals in EU countries to meet, train, and forge esprit de corps and links with other groups—in a word, to coalesce a ragtag collection of activists into a cohesive and disciplined organization. It is becoming far more difficult to get organized and maintain communications with leaders within and outside the country. A specific dimension of al Qaeda was its "veteran's solidarity":

many young radicals, who met first as a group of "buddies" in a Western country, turned into an efficient cell only after having lived in Afghanistan or after being led by someone who had been in Afghanistan and returned. Moreover, a distinctive pattern of al Qaeda was that personal links between veterans of the Afghan jihad had turned into an efficient but flexible chain of command, which is obviously no longer the case.

As to political problems, the West's "demonizing" of Islam has put the Muslim population in the West on the defensive. Although this demonizing may have turned some individuals more radical, it has convinced most Muslims living in the West to adopt a clearer attitude and to advocate a greater integration into Western societies. European authorities have contributed to isolating the radicals by responding positively, at least in terms of rhetoric, to that quest for recognition and integration. Isolation among and alienation from the European Muslim population is now one of the radicals' main challenges.

As a consequence of these developments, two new patterns of Islamic radicalism will probably develop. The first we may call "franchising." Local groups based on local solidarities—most likely those of neighborhood, extended family, and university—with few or no ties to al Qaeda, will assume the label and act according to what they see as al Qaeda's ideology and strategy. The second will be a quest for allies and support *beyond* the pale of Islamic fundamentalism. Radicals may try to find allies and fellow travelers at the expense of the purity of their ideological message. They could find it among the European ultra-Left or, less probably, the ultra-Right. They could find allies among other "liberation" movements (for instance, ex-Ba'athis in Iraq). Some might even serve as proxies or "gun-holders" for rogue states.

Counterterrorism in Europe

Whatever the differences among the European countries, including their appraisal of U.S. policy, EU members share many elements in common.

First, all European governments are reluctant to drastically alter their legal systems and basic political approaches to terrorism. The reason is that the issue of homeland security was raised and essentially settled a long time ago due to a more "indigenous" terrorism (ETA, IRA, Baader-Meinhof, Action Directe, Brigadi Rossi, and so on). In this sense, the Europeans have a more seasoned and experienced counterterrorism homeland apparatus than do the Americans. In countries where the "Islamic" threat had been identified at least a decade ago (as in France), the security apparatus is rather efficient. The recent crisis has engendered greater cooperation among the different countries, as well as with the United States, in most cases. But this cooperation has not led to the importation of political differences among governments into the security function, partly because procedures are institutionalized and partly because this is not a new concern. This has remained much the case even after the March 2004 train bombings in Madrid.

Second, as far as European countries are concerned, the fight against terrorism is a matter of police and intelligence, not military action. These tools are efficient to the extent that transnational cooperation works. In this sense, the new terrorist threat has accelerated a trend already in existence.

The growing isolation of Islamic radicals in Europe should allow the Europeans to continue with this "soft" approach: police and intelligence services are efficient and will probably be sufficient tools of counterterrorism for Europe. However, such a policy will never totally eradicate terrorism. The European tradition of terrorism and political violence that has forged the experience of the counterterrorist institutions makes it easier for young activists to become violent. Put a little differently, the stigma attached to doing such violent things is relatively weaker. Young guys who want to become radical and seek out some sort of spectacular action to validate their confused and injured manhood will not be stopped by this soft approach. Even concentrating on root causes—on the sociology and motivations of the radicals—while important for understanding the radicals' mode of recruitment, will be of little use in drying up the ground on which these radicals prosper. The aim of European policy is not eradication; it is making terrorism a residual factor that can be lived with.

Such a "soft" approach is sustainable in Europe only under one condition: that Islamic radicalism remains a fringe movement. The real danger is in Islamic radicalism enlarging its social base or connecting with other potentially radical movements or governments. The challenge is not to go at the roots of terrorism, as European government spokespeople never tire of saying, for that is well-nigh impossible and will not eradicate terrorism in any case. The challenge is to prevent the radical fringe from finding a broad political base among the local Muslim population.

To regain their momentum and create that base, Euro-Islamic radicals will have to achieve two strategic goals: mobilize other Muslims and link up with non-Muslim radicals.

Eventually, Euro-Islamic leaders will try to mobilize a sufficient part of the Muslim community to provide shelter, logistics, recruits, reliable communications, and so on. To do that, the activists will have to change their patterns of recruitment, which are currently based on spotting some individuals and taking them out of their social milieu. They will have to engage in a more collective *dawa* ("proselytizing"), which would put them on the same path as many nonpolitical conservative and even fundamentalist organizations (like the Tabligh or the Salafis). Interestingly enough, many radical groups (like the London-based Hizb ul-Tahrir) share the views of al Qaeda but think the latter has been premature to launch jihad. They believe that one should first mobilize the Muslim community through intensive proselytizing and political activity.

Eventually, too, Islamist leaders will probably try to establish some sort of joint venture with the remnants of the European extreme Left who share the same hatred for "imperialism." Converts may play a particularly significant role here. Let us not forget that Carlos the Jackal himself converted to Islam in jail and is now praising Osama bin Laden to the hilt.

Pushing for a "Western" Islam

The key issue is thus the attitude of the Muslim population in Europe toward radicalism and terrorism. And for three main reasons, the Muslim population in Europe is a far larger political stake, and plays a far greater political role, than the Muslim population in the United States.

First, unlike the United States, Muslim migrants are the main source of immigration in Europe. Second, that migration originates from the close neighboring southern countries. Legal immigration to the United States is far more diverse in its origins. Third, that migration has created the bulk of the underclass and jobless youth. (In the United States, migrants want to find, and generally do find, jobs that make them quickly upwardly mobile.)

The social, geographic, political, and strategic implications of Muslim immigration to Europe are intertwined. In that light, European countries should pursue a double objective: isolate the Islamic radicals with the support of their own Muslim population, and seek out at least the neutrality of the nonviolent conservative fundamentalists among them. Two different approaches have been in competition in Europe in this regard. The *multiculturalist* approach, tried mainly in Great Britain, treats Muslims as a minority group that should be addressed collectively and that should possibly benefit from a specific status. The *integrationist* approach, which describes that of France, seeks to grant full citizenship to Muslims as individuals but not to consider them as a separate community under any ethnic, cultural, or religious paradigm.

Neither approach seems to be working all that well. The multicultural approach tends to create ghettos. In Great Britain, the Dobson Report (2001) advised the government to stop pushing in this direction and to adapt a more integrative approach. The integrationist approach, however, ignores the quest for a new identity among uprooted Muslims. In France, amid an ongoing debate, the government has decided to establish an official representation of Muslims as a faith group, but not as a cultural or ethnic minority.

However awkwardly, a common approach is slowly emerging in Europe—dealing with the Muslim population in purely religious terms. Encouraging the emergence of a European Islam will help integrate the Muslims, weaken links with foreign countries, and provide a Western-compatible religious identity. The problem thus far is that some governments (like that of France), as well as the bulk of public opinion, equate European Islam with "liberal" Islam. Calling on the Muslims to adapt the basic tenets of Islam to the Western concept of a religion is a mistake.

For example, to officially sponsor "good and liberal" Muslims would be a sort of kiss of death. It would deprive such liberal organizations and leaders of any legitimacy. Besides, the main motivation for youth radicalization is not theological, because youth is not interested in a theological debate. Instead, political radicalization is the main driving force. Moreover, modern secular states should not regulate theology as a matter of policy.

Is there a better approach? Yes. Genuine pluralism is the best way to avoid confrontation with a tight-knit Muslim community. Conservative and even fundamentalist views of religion are manageable in a plural environment, as shown by a host of Protestant, Catholic, and Jewish cases. A pluralistic approach allows civil society to reach the cadres of youth who could be ideal targets for radicals and neofundamentalist groups.

State policy should be based on integration and even "notabilization" of Muslims and community leaders on a pluralistic basis. The priority should be to weaken the links with foreign elements by pushing for the "nativization" of Islam and for preventing the deepening of the ghetto syndrome. Transparency should be the aim.

If that general proposition is accepted, then certain proposals seem to follow logically. First, there should be much tighter control on fund-raising and subsidizing from abroad, which also means better access to open domestic fund-raising and subsidies (for building mosques, for example). Second, governments should establish more links between Islamic religious teaching institutions and the university and academe. Third, religious representation should be encouraged without monopoly. Fourth, mainstream political parties should court and enlist Muslim leaders. Fifth, social policy must avoid confronting Muslims with black-and-white choices. It must, instead, work to let Muslim youth experience a diversity of opinions in line with the spectrum of political diversity in the West.

In this sense, the debate on the issue of supporting or not supporting the U.S. military campaign in Iraq has had a positive impact. In Great Britain, as well in France and elsewhere in Europe, Muslims did not feel isolated or targeted; rather, they felt as though they belonged to mainstream public opinion. In this sense at least, in the European context, the debate between so-called old and new Europe has superseded the debate on the "clash of civilizations."

Such a policy of encouraging pluralism will meet the aspirations of mainstream Muslims in Europe—Islam recognized as a Western religion, Muslims as full citizens—while avoiding the creation of a closed community, ghettos, and minority status. This policy will contribute to the isolation of the terrorists and prevent them from building a dangerous political constituency. Approaches that by design or error drive Muslim communities inward and into themselves will backfire, to the regret of all concerned.

8 | Saudi Arabia and the War on Terrorism

F. Gregory Gause III

The starting point for an effective approach toward Saudi Arabia in the war on terrorism is an accurate diagnosis of just what role the country has played in the growth of al Qaeda and Sunni Muslim extremism. Exaggeration of that role has become so common in the United States that it threatens to destroy a relationship that, though troubled, is essential to American national interests in the Middle East, in the fight against terrorism, and in the world oil market.

The next step is a realistic policy prescription that deals with the problems emanating from Saudi Arabia. The policy prescription must emphasize those areas where tangible progress can be made and must avoid, to the greatest extent possible, unintended consequences that would damage American interests.

Diagnosis

An accurate understanding of Wahhabism is the crucial first step in diagnosing the Saudi role in the global war on terrorism. This is not simply a semantic issue or an arcane exegesis of Islamic texts. Many in the United States contend that Wahhabism is itself the root of Sunni Muslim violence and terrorism.[1] In their appendix to the Congressional Joint Committee report on the September 11 attacks, Senators Jon Kyl and Pat Roberts refer to Wahhabism as "a radical, anti-American variant of Islam."[2] Senators Kyl and Charles Schumer later wrote that Wahhabism "seeks our society's destruction."[3]

If this were true, then we would have no choice but to treat Saudi Arabia as we treated the Taliban regime in Afghanistan, because Saudi Arabia is certainly a Wahhabi state. However, these views misunderstand both Wahhabism itself and its centrality in the growth of violent Sunni Muslim extremist groups.

The puritanical version of Islam preached by Muhammad ibn Abd al-Wahhab in central Arabia in the eighteenth century, which served as the animating ideology for the Al-Saud family's efforts to build a state in Arabia, is not very attractive to most outside observers. It is literalist in its desire to replicate the milieu of the Prophet Muhammad in every possible way. It is extremely intolerant of other interpretations of Islam, particularly Shiism. It is wary and suspicious of non-Muslims. Its views on the role of women in society run counter to inter-

1. The first and most influential post–September 11 book to make this claim is Stephen Schwartz, *The Two Faces of Islam: The House of Sa'ud from Tradition to Terror* (New York: Doubleday, 2002).

2. "Additional Views—Senator Jon Kyl, Senator Pat Roberts," http://news.findlaw.com/hdocs/docs/911rpt/addviewsmem.pdf, p. 20.

3. Jon Kyl and Charles Schumer, "Saudi Arabia's Teachers of Terror," *Washington Post*, August 18, 2003.

national norms, to say the least. It is also hostile to the canons of modern science with some Saudi clerics holding, to this day, that the world is flat and at the center of the solar system.

But none of this is new. Wahhabism has been the official interpretation of Islam in the Saudi domain since the founding of the modern state at the outset of the twentieth century. It has not been a barrier to a very close Saudi-American relationship over the past decades. The phenomenon of anti-American terror in the Sunni Muslim community is much more recent. If this terror were grounded solely in Wahhabism, it should have manifested itself much earlier and should have prevented the historically close Saudi-American relationship.

Wahhabism, as it has developed in Saudi Arabia, is a state ideology, not a revolutionary creed. As retrograde as it might be on social issues, Wahhabism's official arbiters counsel loyalty to the ruler, not revolution. They accord the ruler wide latitude to conduct foreign affairs. Leading Wahhabi scholars and clerics, for example, publicly gave their seal of approval to both the invitation of American forces to Saudi Arabia in 1990 and the use of Saudi Arabia as a base for the 1991 attack on Iraq. They have vehemently rejected the bin Ladenist logic of violence, condemning the attacks of September 11, the bombings in Riyadh in May and November 2003, and the surge of terrorist violence thereafter. Even Wahhabi clerics deeply critical of American policy in the Middle East and of the Saudi-American relationship have spoken out against bin Laden and the violence that he and his followers have perpetrated.[4]

One reason that many have equated "bin Ladenism" with Wahhabism is that bin Laden himself claims to follow the "true" Wahhabi line. He calls for the overthrow of the Saudi

---

4. See F. Gregory Gause III, "Be Careful What You Wish For: The Future of U.S.-Saudi Relations," *World Policy Journal* 49, no. 1 (Spring 2002).

regime and condemns the official clerics for deviating from that line. But allowing bin Laden to define Wahhabism is like allowing the militia movement in the United States to define what it means to be a patriotic American. We should not be taken in by such claims.

Violent anti-American Sunni extremism, personified by bin Laden, is the product of a much more contemporary and complicated set of ideological trends and political experiences. Wahhabism is a part of that mix, but only a part. The crucible of the development of bin Ladenism was the jihad against the Soviet Union in Afghanistan in the 1980s. Among the Arab volunteers there, the retrograde social views and theological intolerance of Saudi Wahhabism came to be blended with the revolutionary political doctrines developed in the 1960s by Muslim Brotherhood thinkers, particularly in Egypt. It is no accident that bin Laden's chief lieutenant in al Qaeda is an Egyptian, Ayman al-Zawahiri, who was prominent in the violent fringes of Egyptian Islamist movements of the 1970s and 1980s. This ideological mélange was filtered through the jihad's success, which was taken as no less than a divine sanction for the political message that developed out of it. Imbued with this confidence, the "Arab Afghans" returned to continue the jihad against their "insufficiently Muslim" governments in Algeria, Egypt, Jordan, and, to a lesser extent, Saudi Arabia. It is only with their failure to remake the politics of the region that, in the mid-1990s, bin Laden began to focus his jihad explicitly against the United States.

Meanwhile, the success in Afghanistan brought a new luster to the concept of jihad in Saudi Arabia (and many other Muslim countries). The Saudi government had encouraged public support for the Afghan jihad (as had the American government). Jihad became a more prominent part of many Saudis' understanding of Islam. Muslims were also "oppressed," as Saudis saw it, by non-Muslims in places like Bosnia, Kashmir, Chechnya, and the West Bank and Gaza. If jihad worked in Afghanistan to free a Muslim population from non-Muslim rule, why should it not work in these other places?

Some of these causes received more official support in Saudi Arabia than others. Bosnian and Palestinian Muslims received much largesse. Saudi diplomatic relations with Russia and India, however, put limits on official support for the Chechen and Kashmiri jihads. But it is undeniable that the Saudi government not only did not oppose the developing jihadist subculture in the country but in some ways encouraged it.

Here is the true intersection in the 1990s between the bin Ladenist movement and Saudi Arabia. Bin Laden himself had been expelled from the country and stripped of his citizenship in 1994. His movement in the country seemed to be rolled up in the mid-1990s, after large-scale arrests. But al Qaeda was active in these other jihadi movements and, in time, was able to make common cause with, or take over, Saudi-funded organizations active in these causes.[5]

5. There are persistent charges that members of the Saudi ruling family either directly or indirectly cut a deal with bin Laden, at minimum promising not to impede his fund-raising and recruiting in Saudi Arabia, perhaps even supporting him financially, in exchange for al Qaeda refraining from targeting Saudi Arabia. The major published source to raise this charge is Gerald Posner, *Why America Slept: The Failure to Prevent 9/11* (New York: Random House, 2003). Nothing in the public record supports this charge. The car bomb attack on the American training mission to the Saudi National Guard in Riyadh in November 1995, which killed seven and wounded sixty, was perpetrated by Saudis who, before their execution, publicly identified bin Laden as their inspiration. However, it is impossible to disprove the charge as well. In the past, Saudi leaders have attempted to buy off foreign opponents, and the ruling family is large enough that it is possible that some prince or group of princes took it upon themselves to explore this option. The most that can be said with certainty is that, if there ever were such an agreement, it did not work very well for the Al-Saud.

It is this intersection that highlights the most important role of Saudi Arabia in the spread of Sunni Islamist extremism. Saudi funding sources, developed during the Afghan jihad and maintained through the 1990s, either wittingly or unwittingly came to support al Qaeda and groups like it. The new prominence of jihad in Saudi Arabia came to be transmitted through Saudi-supported Islamic international organizations (like the Islamic Conference Organization) and nongovernmental organizations (like the World Muslim League and the World Assembly of Muslim Youth) to the rest of the Muslim world. The spread of the jihadist subculture clearly facilitated al Qaeda recruitment and created an atmosphere in which sympathy for al Qaeda could grow. Saudi recruitment channels for jihadis at home, developed in the 1980s to send young Saudis to Afghanistan and continuing in the 1990s to other areas, came to be exploited by al Qaeda to recruit Saudis directly into the organization.

Funding, ideological legitimation, and recruitment are the areas where Saudi Arabia played a key role in developing Sunni Muslim extremism. But that is a far cry from claiming that the Saudi government itself, directly and wittingly, boosted bin Laden and his views. It is even a farther cry from the theories that the Al-Saud were behind September 11, theories on a par with those holding the CIA or the Israeli Mossad responsible for those atrocities. The reality is challenge enough; no good purpose is served by marketing error and delusion.

Prescription

Funding, ideological legitimation, and recruitment are precisely the areas that American foreign policy should target in its policy toward Saudi Arabia in the war on terrorism. In all of these areas, the United States is today dealing with a Saudi government that is usually, though not always, willing to cooperate. The level of cooperation has varied, in part because not all elements of the Saudi regime have been equally committed to that cooperation.

A number of factors contribute to that reluctance, including tensions over the direction of American Middle East policy in general and very clear differences between the two countries regarding the definition of *terrorism* as it relates to the Arab-Israeli conflict. However, the key to Saudi reluctance is the domestic political costs of confronting a movement that had considerable sympathy within Saudi Arabia for many of its goals if not its tactics. Being against Islam is not a winning position in Saudi politics. The fact that any cooperation with the United States would be seen by many as bowing to American pressure, when (from the late 1990s) the United States has been profoundly unpopular in Saudi Arabia, has furnished further disincentive.

However, the attacks on the United States on September 11, 2001, and on the housing compounds in Riyadh on May 12 and November 9, 2003, led to new levels of seriousness on the part of the Saudi authorities in addressing the problem of Sunni extremism that they had, however unwittingly, helped to create. These events brought home to the Saudi leadership, more quickly to some than to others, the threat posed by Sunni Muslim extremism to the domestic stability of their own regime.

On the funding issue, American pressure and the Saudi realization of the seriousness of the threat have led to important steps by Riyadh to exercise more control over Saudi-supported charities and to monitor financial transactions from the kingdom. During 2002, the Saudi government took several steps in this direction, including requiring Foreign Ministry approval of any charitable project undertaken outside the country, ordering audits of Saudi charities, and establishing new oversight bodies in the government to monitor charities.[6] After the May 2003 bombings Riyadh moved to close ten of the foreign offices of the al-Haramain Foundation, frequently cited as a conduit of funds for extremist groups, after earlier closing the foundation's offices in Bosnia and Somalia.[7]

The task for American foreign policy is to hold the Saudi government's feet to the fire on this issue, pushing it to follow up on its own declared policy. The Bush administration has been doing so, dispatching in August 2003 a team of senior counterterrorist officials to press the Saudis.[8] Just a few weeks later, the Saudi cabinet adopted new regulations against money laundering, and the Saudi government allowed the IRS and FBI to establish a permanent liaison office in Riyadh to coordinate with Saudi counterparts.[9] A practical step in this direction would be to press the Saudis to actually create the Saudi Higher Authority for Relief and Charity Work, a step that had been announced but not implemented, to serve as the oversight body for all charitable organizations and associations offering services outside the country.[10]

In December 2003, Saudi sources at the embassy in Wash-

6. *Al-Hayat*, March 21, 2002, 1, 6; John Mintz, "Saudis Deny Dragging Feet on Terrorism," *Washington Post*, December 4, 2002.

7. John Mintz, "Wahhabi Strain of Islam Faulted," *Washington Post*, June 27, 2003.

8. Susan Schmidt, "U.S. Officials Press Saudis on Aiding Terror," *Washington Post*, August 6, 2003.

9. "Cabinet OK's anti-money laundering legislation," *Arab News*, August 19, 2003; "U.S. and Saudis Join in Anti-Terror Effort," *New York Times*, August 26, 2003.

10. As of late May 2003, the body had yet to be established, according to the Saudi response to questions posed by the Counter-Terrorism Committee of the UN Security Council. The reference to the body is on page 11 of the response, Counter-Terrorism Committee document S/2003/583.

ington revealed that the Saudi government intends to stop providing diplomatic status for Islamic clerics and educators preaching and teaching overseas. These sources also claimed an intent to "shut down the Islamic affairs section in every embassy."[11] If this actually occurs, it will be a significant step and a major signal of change in Saudi policy.

While many in Washington remain skeptical of the Saudi commitment in this area, some appear to have become too complacent. It still makes sense to pressure Riyadh to demonstrate its good intentions rather than to assume they either will or will not follow through on recent initiatives. If further cooperation is not forthcoming, the United States should not hesitate to "name and shame" Saudi individuals and organizations involved in the deliberate financing of al Qaeda and affiliate groups.

One area of particular sensitivity in the issue of funding is Saudi support, official and private, for Hamas, the Palestinian Islamist group officially designated as a terrorist organization by the United States. There is no question that Saudi money goes to Hamas organizations and projects.[12] Pushing the Saudis to end as much of that support as they can would be valuable, but the negative consequences of making the Hamas issue a very high-profile public part of Saudi-American relations are considerable. In terms of Saudi public opinion, equating al Qaeda and Hamas does not delegitimate the latter; it legitimates the former. Better for Washington to separate the al Qaeda issue from the Hamas issue by pushing publicly and privately for absolute cooperation on the former and

11. See Susan Schmidt and Caryle Murphy, "U.S. Revokes Visa of Cleric at Saudi Embassy," *Washington Post*, December 7, 2003.

12. Adil al-Jubeir, foreign affairs adviser to Crown Prince Abdallah, has admitted as much. David R. Sands, "Kingdom Moves Against Terrorism," *Washington Times*, June 13, 2003. See also Matthew Levitt, "Who Pays for Palestinian Terror?" *The Weekly Standard*, August 25, 2003.

keeping the latter in the realm of private diplomacy, at least while al Qaeda remains America's foremost priority.

On legitimation, Washington has a less public role to play than on funding. The U.S. government will not be successful in telling Muslims what Islam is, and it should not try to do so. Here, the key is to press the Saudis to use their considerable ideological resources, both at home and in the Muslim world in general, to place bin Laden, his actions, and his interpretation of Islam outside the pale of acceptable Muslim discourse. This requires the Saudis to confront head-on the jihadist subculture that they indirectly nurtured during the past two decades.

As in the funding area, the Saudis have recently demonstrated a willingness to take on this task. In late May 2003, after the bombings in Riyadh, the Saudi Ministry of Islamic Affairs announced the removal of 353 religious officials from their positions (because they lacked the "qualifications" to work in mosques) and the requirement that 1,357 religious officials undergo further training.[13] Immediately after September 11, leading Saudi religious officials condemned the attacks and, since then, have consistently and publicly rejected bin Laden's interpretation of jihad. A recent example was the statement of the Higher Council of Ulama in August 2003, reaffirming that violent attacks on innocents "are criminal acts . . . not jihad in the path of God." The council called on the Saudi authorities to bring before the courts any scholar who issues a fatwa ("religious judgment") approving of such acts.[14] Continuing efforts by the Saudis in this direction, not only at home but also through the Islamic intergovernmental and nongovernmental organizations that they fund, are essential.

13. *Al-Hayat*, May 28, 2003, 1, 6.
14. *Al-Hayat*, August 17, 2003, 1, 6.

On recruitment, the Saudis need to police much more stringently the networks of al Qaeda members and sympathizers that have developed within the kingdom itself. For too long, even after September 11, Riyadh refused to face up to this issue. Just days before the May 2003 bombing, the country's chief security official, Interior Minister Prince Na'if, termed the al Qaeda presence in the country as "weak and almost nonexistent."[15] Since the bombing, Saudi security forces have been much more aggressive in efforts to root out al Qaeda. In the aftermath of the May and November 2003 bombings, more than six hundred Saudis were arrested. There have been a number of shootouts between Saudi police and suspected al Qaeda sympathizers, with tens killed on each side, and Saudi security services have discovered a number of substantial arms caches.[16] The United States should urge the Saudis to make a special effort to prevent infiltration by al Qaeda sympathizers and other Islamist militants across the long and largely unguarded Saudi-Iraqi border.

The Saudis could do more on all of these issues, and the United States should monitor Saudi government actions carefully. There is also the larger issue, beyond the scope of this essay, of the consequences of Wahhabi proselytizing in the Muslim world. Even if the official Saudi interpretation of Islam is not, in and of itself, the wellspring of anti-American terror, its retrograde views on social tolerance, gender issues, and democracy place it at variance with American goals throughout the Muslim world, including in the United States itself. Helping other Muslim countries promote more tolerant and inclusive interpretations of Islam should be part of the

15. Glenn Kessler and Alan Sipress, "Western Targets Bombed in Riyadh," *Washington Post*, May 13, 2003.

16. Neil MacFarquhar, "Al Qaeda Blamed in Deadly Attack on Saudi Homes," *New York Times*, November 10, 2003.

American foreign policy agenda, to the extent that Washington can help on these issues. But on the specific issue of anti-American terrorism, there is a clear willingness, more pronounced since the May 2003 bombings, on the part of the Saudi government to cooperate with Washington. That is a basis upon which to build.

Do No Harm

The United States should avoid superficially appealing policies toward Saudi Arabia that will redound to our disadvantage. In particular, Washington should suppress its natural tendency to believe that more democracy will make things better in foreign countries.

Democratic elections in Saudi Arabia would reflect the very strong anti-Americanism now prevalent in the country. A Gallup poll, conducted in late January–early February 2002, reported that 64 percent of Saudi respondents viewed the United States either very unfavorably or most unfavorably. Majorities in the poll associated America with the adjectives "conceited, ruthless and arrogant." Fewer than 10 percent saw the United States as either friendly or trustworthy.[17] A Zogby International poll, conducted in March 2002, reported similar results. Only 30 percent of the Saudis polled supported American-led efforts to fight terrorism, while 57 percent opposed them.[18] A subsequent Zogby poll, conducted in July 2003, found that 70 percent of the Saudis polled had an unfavorable impression of the United States, with only 24 percent having a favorable impression.[19] An elected Saudi legislature, for

17. Richard Burkholder, "The U.S. and the West—Through Saudi Eyes," *Gallup Tuesday Briefing*, August 6, 2002.
18. "The 10 Nation 'Impressions of America' Poll Report," Zogby International, August 7, 2002.
19. www.zogby.com/news/ReadNews.dbm?ID=725.

example, would put pressure on the Saudi government to cooperate *less*, not more, with the United States in the war on terrorism and on general Middle East issues.

Saudi anti-Americanism is not an immutable fact. It reflects the tensions in the relationship since September 11, the negative reactions to American attacks on Afghanistan and Iraq, and the collapse of the Arab-Israeli peace process. But it can change with time, as regional realities change. However, a push for democracy in Saudi Arabia now would not serve American interests. President Bush cannot take back what he said at the National Endowment for Democracy on November 6, 2003, but he can selectively implement his vision. And he should. Cautious steps from the Saudis themselves to broaden the scope of political participation in their society, such as the October 2003 announcement of plans for municipal elections to fill half the seats of the proposed municipal councils, should be welcomed. Washington should not push for countrywide elections to national institutions, such as the Consultative Council (an appointed body).

The United States must also avoid the temptation to simply throw up its hands and declare the Saudis an enemy. This impulse is based on a faulty reading of the role of Wahhabism and Saudi Arabia in the development of Sunni Islamist extremism, as discussed earlier. Beyond that, the temptation seems to be an emotionally satisfying thought for many who see Wahhabism, the monarchy, the treatment of women, the Saudi stance on Arab-Israeli issues, and various other elements of Saudi society and governance as so antithetical to American principles that our country should have no truck with the House of Saud. As in so many things in life, however, what temporarily satisfies our emotional needs would not be good for us in the long run.

Those who urge such a policy fail the basic test of practical politics: They offer no alternative to the Saudi-American rela-tionship.[20] They are extremely fuzzy on what Washington should do the day after it declares Saudi Arabia an enemy. Military invasion and occupation of the oil fields? Given how difficult and expensive U.S. occupation of Iraq has become, this cannot be a serious option. Those who advocate "regime change" in Riyadh, through greater democracy or direct U.S. action, can offer no assurances that a new regime would be any friendlier to the United States, harder on Islamist extrem-ists, or more in tune with global human rights norms than the incumbents.

The plain fact is that not only do the rulers of Riyadh sit on 25 percent of all the world's known conventional oil reserves, but they also control the Muslim holy cities of Mecca and Medina, the focal point of faith for 1.4 billion Muslims in the world. Surely having a government there that, despite its problems, responds to American pressures on oil questions and the war on terrorism is better for American interests than the leap into the dark that military occupation or regime change would represent. Looking around the region, it is bet-ter than several other easily imaginable alternatives as well.

20. Argued in Adam Garfinkle, "Weak Realpolitik: The Vicissitudes of Saudi Bashing," *The National Interest*, no. 67 (Spring 2002).

9 | With Allies Like This: Pakistan and the War on Terrorism

Stephen Philip Cohen

During his 1999–2000 presidential campaign, George W. Bush could not name the leader of Pakistan. In June 2003, President (and army chief) Pervez Musharraf spent a high-profile day at Camp David, where a multiyear $3 billion American aid package was announced. We learn from this little anecdote that the September 11 attacks on the United States have propelled Pakistan into the limelight of U.S. national security concerns. There it remains today, labeled a "frontline ally" in the war on terrorism.[1]

To some extent, this recent contretemps repeats an old pattern of alliance and estrangement that has characterized

I thank Mr. Moeed Yusuf for his assistance in writing this chapter.

1. The term "terrorism" is defined differently by many people—we treat it as attacks on unarmed civilians; a perfected definition would term it a hatred that finds an expression in violence, often designed to shock and horrify.

U.S.-Pakistan relations since the early 1950s.[2] Pakistan was, in turn, an instrument of American policy in containing the Soviets and then the Chinese and then in removing the Soviets from Afghanistan. However, this time there is a difference: Pakistan is a critical ally, but it is also a potential source of terrorism, as well as a declared nuclear weapons state. Some have pointed to Pakistan's growing social extremism, its use of terror as an instrument of state policy in Kashmir, its continuing meddling in Afghanistan, and evidence of leakage of Pakistani nuclear technology to Iran, North Korea, and perhaps other states. If Pakistan is an ally as far as Afghanistan is concerned, it has not behaved like a friend of the United States in many other respects.

A closer look at Pakistan reveals that radical groups do not enjoy widespread support in the country. Despite recent electoral trends, most middle-class and urban Pakistanis do not subscribe to the radical agenda. They believe Pakistan should be a modern but Islamic state—with "Islamic" being confined to a few spheres of public life.

Nonetheless, Pakistan today finds itself at a critical juncture. Radical Islam has found a home in Pakistan, and the danger of the spread of extremism, though by no means imminent, is greater than it was a decade ago. Pakistan is also one of the world's most anti-American countries, which makes Americans especially vulnerable there.[3] If its radicalism

2. For an outstanding overview of the relationship, see Dennis Kux, *The United States and Pakistan, 1947–2000: Disenchanted Allies* (Washington, D.C.: Woodrow Wilson Center Press, 2001).

3. Graham Fuller notes that there is widespread unfavorable opinion of the United States in the Muslim world (53%) with less than half of that (22%) holding a positive view. He states that anti-American perception is the highest in Pakistan, Iran, and Saudi Arabia. Graham E. Fuller, "The Youth Factor: The New Demographics of the Middle East and Implications for U.S. Policy," *Brookings Project on U.S. Policy Towards the Islamic World*, Analysis Paper 3, July 2003, 22–25.

is left unchecked, Pakistan could indeed evolve into a nuclear-armed terrorist state. Washington must seize the opportunity presented by its current alliance to help move Pakistan in the direction of moderation and stability.

To do this requires a policy of engagement on two parallel tracks. The first is short-term and "curative," ensuring that Pakistan's present terrorist groups are checked by better police, army, and intelligence operations and addressing the specific causes that motivate their acts. The second policy track is "preventive," a long-term engagement to revitalize Pakistan's enfeebled civilian and social institutions. This second track is a daunting but essential task.

Typologies of Terrorism

Terrorism in Pakistan has several dimensions. Three distinct types can be distinguished.

Type I concerns terrorism in Afghanistan and is the focus of the new American relationship with Pakistan, which derives primarily from the latter's importance in combating al Qaeda and the Taliban. Pakistan has been cooperative in rounding up al Qaeda cadres but much less obliging about the Taliban, which receives significant support from Pakistani Pashtuns and some of Pakistan's Islamist parties. In all, about five hundred al Qaeda members have been captured by the Pakistanis and turned over to the United States.

Type II terrorism is Pakistan's direct and indirect support for Kashmir-related groups that have attacked Indian forces and innocent civilians. A few such groups seem to be intent on precipitating a war between Delhi and Islamabad and oppose the latter government because it abandoned the Taliban and reversed course on Afghanistan.[4]

4. These Kashmir-specific groups may have a wider reach. A group was

Type III terrorism in Pakistan refers to the domestic dimension. Many of Pakistan's terrorists are sectarian, and some have links to one or another group operating in Kashmir/India and Afghanistan. A number of these groups have links to various Pakistani political parties, Islamabad's intelligence services, or the army. In the past, the state had used some of these groups for domestic purposes.[5]

Pakistanis do not necessarily perceive terrorism in one location in the same way as they perceive it in another location. Although sectarian violence is stigmatized, the use of terrorism in Kashmir is widely seen as a legitimate last resort in the Kashmiri "freedom struggle"—although this struggle is never called terrorism. This difference in view complicates any strategy to deal with one kind of terrorism, for the types overlap in practice. In addition, some groups are involved in more than one kind of terrorism.

The Curative Track

An American policy designed to curb existing terrorism in Pakistan should deal with all three types. But America should take care not to get preoccupied with Type I terrorism while ignoring the other two. Along the curative track, three policies recommend themselves.

First, there should be continued support to improve the professionalism of Pakistan's police forces, which are notori-

---

charged in northern Virginia as being part of a Lashkar-e-Toiba cell and accused of plotting attacks on a "friendly country" (i.e. India); at least two of the eight arrested were Pakistani nationals, with others being born in Pakistan. *Dawn*, June 28, 2003.

5. Examples of such groups include Jaish-e-Muhammad, Sipah-e-Sahaba Pakistan, and Lashkar-e-Jhangvi Pakistan.

ous for their abuse of power. The police are viewed by most citizens as predators, not protectors, and support for terrorist groups is often a by-product of alienation from the Pakistani state. For its part, the Pakistani government should ensure that the police receive salaries and support commensurate with their grave responsibilities; in the long run, this expenditure is more important for the security and stability of Pakistan than money spent on advanced weapons and military hardware.

Second, because the Pakistani army remains politically important, Washington should link the quantity and quality of *military assistance* to Pakistan to good performance in countering all three kinds of terrorist groups. The effort should begin, obviously, with the first category but should eventually include the second and third, as well. Many steps have been discussed between American and Pakistani officials in this regard, including exerting greater control over the *madrassas*, providing closer surveillance of suspect groups, shutting down terrorist training camps, improving surveillance along the Line of Control in Kashmir, and countering extremist propaganda. If Pakistan demonstrates vigor and competence in such matters, military aid and cooperation from the United States should be increased.

Finally, the United States should address the two major foreign policy issues that are the focus of some Pakistani terrorists and that give them broader legitimacy. Pakistan's movement against terrorists operating in Kashmir will have to be linked to progress in a peace process with India. Absent such progress, Pakistan will not unilaterally strip itself of a vital, if provocative and risky, policy instrument. The United States must notch up its engagement in the region and promote a peace process between the two countries, even if this process is disguised as "facilitation."[6] American support for a peace process, which has as a major component the well-being of the Kashmiri people, will blunt one of the "causes" of radical Islamists. Such a process will meet with strong resistance from the radical Pakistanis and may well include violence and terrorism designed to disrupt it. However, engagement is essential, not only for long-term U.S. interests but also for the stability of the Pakistani state.

Similarly, any comprehensive policy toward Pakistan must address Pakistan's relationship with Afghanistan. The two states have a long and complex relationship that took an astonishing turn when American forces removed the Taliban government with Pakistan's help. Despite recent events, there remains sympathy for the Taliban and al Qaeda among the Pakistani Pashtuns. Radical Islamic groups in Pakistan's North-West Frontier Province are especially attuned to developments in Afghanistan. A continuing U.S. presence next door, without any tangible positive results for the Afghan people, will further intensify grievances in Pakistan.

The best American policy is one of prevention: ensuring that Afghanistan does not collapse into chaos and that Pakistan remains supportive of the Hamid Karzai regime. The United States needs to advance the effective neutralization of Afghanistan in the region as it helps Afghans to rebuild the country from within. Clearly, Afghanistan needs substantial and long-term outside assistance to help manage its own security. Washington should actively support the process, with the

---

6. American officials vehemently rejected "facilitation" at one point but now accept it as a legitimate American role. Secretary of State Powell mentioned the matter in a September 5, 2003, speech at George Washington University. The Council on Foreign Relations, in a forthcoming report, will recommend the appointment of a high-level American facilitator based in the White House.

knowledge that the greatest danger of an Afghan collapse might be the radicalization of large parts of Pakistan.

To summarize, nothing will happen if America merely demands an end to Pakistani support for terrorist groups. The United States must also offer positive inducements in the form of additional aid to Pakistan, political support for a dialogue with India, and assurance of a friendly and stable Afghanistan.

All this is absolutely necessary, but not sufficient. Washington must also move beyond short-term cures to address the deeper causes of radicalism and terrorism in Pakistan. That brings us to the preventive track.

The Preventive Track

The second policy track the United States needs to follow in Pakistan should focus on the mushrooming growth of extremism from which terrorists of several sorts are recruited. Pakistan is not an inherently extremist Islamic country. Despite its having reared some prominent Islamist theorists, it is not like Saudi Arabia, whose form of Salafi Islam is organic to its state formation. Pakistan's radical groups are a mixed lot. Some are criminals trying to wrap themselves in the mantle of divine justice. Some have modest, Pakistan-related objectives. Some are seized with sectarian hatred. A few are internationalist apocalyptical terrorists in tune with the al Qaeda philosophy.

The rise of all radical groups to prominence, however, can in large part be attributed to the patronage they have received from the Pakistan army. Over the years, the army has used these groups as instruments of domestic as well as foreign policy. But although the Pakistani state must bear responsibility for its cultivation of some of these terrorist groups, other problems now overwhelm the question of origins. There is currently increasing frustration with the lack of economic opportunities, the rise in crime and violence (especially against women) and a growing pool of unemployed college students and graduates who are potential supporters of terrorism. Pakistan's adverse educational and demographic trends, its enfeebled institutions, and its stagnant economy will eventually produce a situation where even the army cannot stem the growth of radical Islamism, and might even be captured by it.

To avert such a scenario, Washington must provide support to revitalize Pakistan's core institutions. Pakistan's economy requires an overhaul, its educational system must be reconstructed, and, above all, as political and administrative institutions gain strength, the army must curb its meddling in political affairs. Let us look at these three areas in turn.

The Economy

Since the 1999 coup, international assistance, close monitoring of expenditures, and consistent policies have produced a modest economic recovery in Pakistan. The country has moved away from default, but it still has a large international debt, and both unemployment and underemployment remain high.[7] America should continue to support the economy with macro-level assistance. Continued (and even expanded) economic aid, however, should be linked to several key policy changes.

One such change is that the Pakistani people must see tangible evidence that its government's tilt in favor of the United States brings significant benefits to all layers of society and all corners of the country. Most U.S. aid is invisible to the average

---

7. For an assessment of prospects, see "Pakistan Plans $500 Million Return to Bond Market," *Financial Times*, June 20, 2003.

Pakistani, who cares little about debt relief or balance of payment problems. Without being obtrusive or boasting, the message should be that America is vitally concerned about Pakistan's economic progress and wants to see the economy adapt to a fast-changing world. Specific projects in the arena of high technology, improving indigenous manufacturing, and research and development capabilities would demonstrate that a globally competitive Pakistan is in America's interest.[8] Further, Washington should encourage American companies to invest in Pakistan in areas that are seen to be important for balanced Pakistani growth, not merely the source of fat profits for a few American companies.[9]

Aid accountability is vital. Benchmarks and guidelines should certainly be negotiated with Pakistani authorities, as usual. But once the terms are agreed upon, economic assistance should be closely monitored to ensure that the funds are not funneled into other purposes and that corruption is kept to a minimum. The United States and other donors have every right to link economic assistance with conditions that ensure that the money is being properly utilized.[10] The essential principle that American aid administrators must keep in mind is that aid is not merely a payoff to a regime; its purpose,

---

8. For an outstanding review of Pakistan's economic and governmental problems, see Dr. Akmal Hussain, *Pakistan: National Human Development Report, 2003* (Islamabad: UNDP, 2003). For a discussion of American economic policy options, see Ambassador Teresita C. Schaffer, *Reviving Pakistan's Economy: A Report from the CSIS Project* (Washington, D.C.: Center for Strategic and International Studies, January 2002).

9. One group of companies to focus on would be those already invested in South Asia: General Electric, Microsoft, and Boeing already have experience in the region, and their products might help break the region's trade barriers.

10. Pakistan has resisted conditionality with the recent aid package. Strong political voices in Pakistan are pushing the government to reject any U.S. aid that comes with strings attached. See "Leghari Asks Govt to Reject US Aid With Strings: Congressmen's Bias Flayed," *Dawn*, July 29, 2003.

in this case, is to help that regime make the structural changes that will prevent Pakistan from evolving into a dangerous state.

Education

Both the American and Pakistani governments are aware of the collapse of Pakistan's educational system, but they tend to look at different aspects of the problem. Washington has focused on the *madrassas*, the religious schools that are perceived to be teaching terror and preaching hatred toward the West.[11] Islamabad emphasizes the importance of improving advanced technical education and, thus, has started another scheme to massively train scientists and technicians.

While the United States must continue pressuring Pakistani authorities to revamp the *madrassa* system, as President Musharraf has promised to do, the agenda should not be confined to this dimension alone. The predominance of the *madrassas* in Pakistan is a consequence of the massive infusion of foreign, largely Saudi, funds for the conservative *madrassas* and of the Pakistani state's failure to provide adequate educational facilities to begin with.[12] If modern educational institutions are not revitalized, the *madrassas* will continue to thrive. The new U.S. aid package only allocates $21.5 million to primary education and literacy in 2003, about a tenth of the cost of a single F-22 jet, and much of that will be swallowed up in administrative costs.

---

11. There were only 250 *madrassas* at independence and about 5,000 in the 1980s. This number has now jumped to 45,000, according to some estimates. Those that preach hatred may only constitute 10 to 15 percent of the total—but few offer an education that prepares their graduates for a modern occupation.

12. For a discussion of the Pakistani *madrassas*, see P. W. Singer, "Pakistan's Madrassahs: Ensuring a System of Education, Not Jihad," *Brookings Project on U.S. Policy Towards the Islamic World*, Analysis Paper 14, November 2001.

At the elementary and secondary education levels, more aid should be provided, but it must be conditional upon actual achievement in literacy levels and teacher training. Indeed, the problem of teacher training is so great that Pakistan should be encouraged to bring in foreign teachers, who will not only provide high levels of technical skill but who will also break down the cultural isolation of many Pakistanis.

At the graduate and postgraduate levels, American educational assistance should focus on restoring the many private institutions that once thrived in Pakistan (including some church-related schools) and on restoring Pakistan's liberal arts, humanities, and social science expertise, which is so necessary for the training of an informed citizenry. The present approach, elevating colleges to the university level, does not address the absence of quality faculty. Where will these instructors come from? A massive increase in the Fulbright program would make sense, as would an emergency training program for Pakistani educational administrators and faculty members. Moreover, Pakistan should follow the lead of Bangladesh and a few other states and send some advanced students to India for technical and nontechnical training.

Perhaps the most important condition that must be put on aid for the educational sector is that the Pakistan government itself should increasingly assume the responsibility for education's funding and administration. The share of government expenditures on education should increase; if it is cut, Pakistan should pay the price in terms of reduced military and economic aid.[13]

Finally, any educational aid program must calibrate the amount of aid relative to the sector's absorptive capacity.

13. Pakistan is showing signs of improvement in this regard. The latest federal budget (FY04) has increased the allocation for education expenditures to 1.05 percent of total expenditures, from 0.9 percent in FY03.

Dedicational aid programs should begin small and increase only when Pakistan's capacity has grown. To reiterate, the essential principle to bear in mind is that this aid is not being given for its own sake but to achieve permanent and positive change in Pakistan.

Democratization

"Democratization" is one of the three benchmarks set forth by President Bush when he announced the 2003 aid package for Pakistan. Washington should encourage the Pakistani army to develop an informal timetable for the restoration of *complete* democracy and to stick to it. This timetable may last for several years, but now is the time to reshape the civil-military balance in Pakistan toward something resembling normalcy.

Although democracy in Pakistan may be difficult to bring about, the best way for the United States to forestall the rise of radical Islam, to safeguard a modicum of civil liberties, and to preempt separatist movements is to insist, as a condition of aid, that the Pakistani government allow the mainstream political parties (the Pakistan Muslim League and the Pakistan People's Party) to function freely.[14] The goal should be a spectrum of Islamic and liberal parties that are willing to operate within a parliamentary context and that are tolerant of sectarian and other minorities. As long as the Pakistani establishment does not tolerate groups, parties, and leaders that have practiced and preached violence within Pakistan and across its borders in India and Afghanistan, the United States should not be concerned about the ideological outlook of the parties. Indeed, avowedly Islamic parties that eschew violence are particularly useful in a Pakistani context; they allow for the

14. In the October 2002 elections, the leaders of both mainstream parties were allowed neither to return to Pakistan nor to compete in the elections.

expression of views whose believers, if excluded from the public realm, might more readily turn to violence and terror.

Finally, Washington must take seriously the fact that Pakistan is an important arena of *ideas*. Most educated Pakistanis are not ideologically anti-American, but they are angry with the United States for changing the regimes in Afghanistan and Iraq and supporting President Musharraf. There is no one telling America's side of the story or engaging its critics in the realm of ideas and public discourse. American information programs in the country are practically nonexistent; these programs need to be revived and vastly expanded, and private organizations must be encouraged to increase their exchange and cultural programs, especially with younger Pakistanis, academics, journalists, and opinion leaders. In the long run the greatest challenge to the United States in Pakistan is in the realm of ideas—the field must not be abandoned to Islamic radicals or those who see the United States as an inherently evil state.

For the Long Haul

Despite its many problems, Pakistan is still one of the freest and most democratic Muslim states, even as it has become an increasingly dangerous one. While the threat from Islamic radicalism in Pakistan is not as high as is perceived by some in the West, the country is poised at a moment where further neglect could accelerate its descent into radicalism, producing a state that threatens regional and global security.

The United States should engage itself with Pakistan over the long haul, not just the short term. It needs to assist Pakistan in curbing the threat from radicalism at home while achieving a more normal relationship with India and Afghanistan. Equally important, the U.S. government should help

Pakistan revitalize its enfeebled institutions and provide its population with much-needed opportunities for growth. The goal should not be to merely sustain a Pakistan that poses no threat but to help develop a stable Pakistan that can become a model for the Islamic world and, perhaps, a partner in establishing a more liberal order in parts of the Middle East and elsewhere. The best way to achieve this goal is to pursue a course of sustained engagement with Pakistan's civil side, breaking with the pattern of engagement and estrangement focusing on the military that characterized the past.

A necessary adjunct to such a policy would have global as well as Pakistan-specific components. A streamlining of laws in the United States to deal with terrorist-related detainees is in order. So is a still clearer message to repeatedly emphasize that the U.S. target in the war on terrorism is not Islam or Pakistanis, but solely terrorism.

There is no assurance that curative or preventive policies will succeed. Both would require active cooperation by the Pakistani government, as well as the support of key elites. Even with their support, some sectors of Pakistani society are so badly run down that a well-funded effort could still fail. However, we will only know this if such an attempt is made. What is certain is that without a concerted effort to curb Islamic radicalism in the short term, and to dry up its recruitment base in the long term, the worst predictions about a rogue, nuclear-armed, terrorist-supporting Pakistan are likely to come true.

10 | American Muslims as Allies in the War on Terrorism

M. A. Muqtedar Khan

Any and every injury to America is as much an injury to American Muslims as it is to any other American. Therefore, the loss of life and property, as well as the erosion of security as a result of the attacks of September 11, 2001, hurt American Muslims as much as they hurt other Americans. More than two hundred American Muslims lost their lives on that fateful day, and many American Muslims have since suffered from the political and economic consequences of the attacks. American Muslims also suffered when America responded, militarily and otherwise, to September 11.

Today, other Americans view the entire American Muslim community with varying degrees of suspicion. The community's institutions are under siege, the status of its civil rights is in grave jeopardy, and many Muslims are suffering socially as well as professionally from rising anti-Muslim sentiments in America. American Muslims have also seen thousands of their fellow Muslims die in wars, which would not have been waged had America not been attacked.

The point is that when America is attacked, American Muslims suffer, and when America responds, American Muslims suffer again. It follows that American Muslims should be more concerned than anyone about essential American security and that they have a compelling incentive to do all they can to make sure that the international war on terrorism is effective and successful. That is not all. In the process of fighting terrorism, the U.S. government has undertaken actions that have raised the level of anti-Americanism worldwide. Perhaps these actions have been fully justified and wise, perhaps not—but there is no question that one side effect has been an antipathy toward the United States of which Americans, in general, are increasingly aware. Arab countries and Muslim organizations in America have tried to manipulate this awareness by trying to get the United States to focus more on the Israeli-Palestinian conflict and less on the war on terrorism, as if doing the former would palpably aid the latter.

The growth of anti-Americanism in non-Muslim societies, especially in western Europe and to a lesser extent in eastern Asia, has become a source of delight to many Muslim commentators overseas. They see it as a vindication of their claims about America's unjust foreign policy and diplomatic heavy-handedness. Unfortunately, some American Muslims also seem to enjoy the rise of anti-Americanism. This is not very smart: Anti-Americanism overseas engenders xenophobia at home, and today nobody is more "foreign" than American Muslims. American Muslims, more than anyone else, will become the victims of xenophobia in America. It is therefore in the interest of American Muslims to work to reverse the growth of anti-Americanism everywhere, particularly in the Muslim world.

American Muslims Need Regime Change

The American Muslim community has not been served well by its national organizations, such as the Council for American Islamic Relations and the American Muslim Council. In the aftermath of September 11, the instinctive response of the leaders of these and other, smaller organizations was to protect the Muslim world from America's revenge. They argued against any military reaction. They also hoped to cash in, quite literally, on the post–September 11 introspection in America, using the rising tempo of concern to raise money. They also sought to bring the Palestinian crisis to the front and center, thinking that enough Americans would blame the Jews for September 11 to force partisan progress on the issue.

All these tactics, and the strategy in general, have backfired. The overall strategy has undermined the credibility of these organizations and has made some of them targets of investigation.

All the major American Muslim organizations failed to condemn either Osama bin Laden or al Qaeda for weeks. They invariably hedged in their public statements by vaguely referring to "whoever was responsible."[1] Many of these organizations encouraged a sense of denial within the community through statements that seemed vague and that even occasionally insinuated that other vested interests may have been responsible for the attacks. This sense of denial, nurtured by ridiculous conspiracy theories that still pervade the Muslim community, has undermined the capacity of many American Muslims to be effective partners in the war on terrorism. It has

1. See Khalid Abou el-Fadl, "US Muslims, Unify and Stand Up," *Los Angeles Times*, July 14, 2002.

also undermined the efforts of liberal Muslims to heal the widening gulf between Americans and American Muslims.

Today the American Muslim community is deeply divided. For purposes of simplicity, we can define one side of the divide as consisting of those Muslims whose top priority is the future of their children and the American Muslim community and the other side as consisting of those whose top priority is advancing the interests of Arab and other Muslim nations, particularly Palestine. Among the American Muslims for the "Muslim world," many are still in deep denial about who was responsible for September 11. They also believe that the United States is knowingly and consciously waging a war on Islam.[2] These Muslims do not recognize the dangers posed by rogue Islamists. These Muslims and some national organizations are more interested in using the American political system to advance back-home causes, even at the expense of the American Muslim community. For them, American Muslims are instruments to be manipulated and used. These groups and individuals do not constitute a significant direct threat to America, but they can and are undermining the efforts of other Muslims who do not share their vision.

In nearly every mosque, every institution, and every forum—and even within families—Muslims "for America" are locked in a struggle with Muslims for the Muslim world to shape the community's direction. There is a silent and slow, but steady, revolution going on within the American Muslim community. More and more, Muslims for America are realizing that their national organizations are funded by foreign

2. According to a survey conducted by Project MAPS at Georgetown University and Zogby International in November/December 2001, only one out of three American Muslims believed that the war on terror was a war on Islam. This figure most certainly has changed since the use of the Patriot Act and the war and occupation of Iraq. To review the survey, go to http://www.projectmaps.com.

sources that have misguided and misrepresented them. Muslims for America are beginning to wake up to the fact that they have been gradually mesmerized by the jihad for Palestine, and they are struggling to break free.[3]

So far, however, American Muslims for the Muslim world remain dominant. Using foreign resources, they have hijacked the voice, the agenda, and even the future of what is, by every measure, an internally diverse American Muslim community. A quick survey of these organizations will immediately expose their misplaced loyalties and priorities.

A visit to the Web site of the Council for American Islamic Relations (CAIR) showed that it was more interested in Daniel Pipes and the issues concerning Iraq and Palestine than with things that affect the future and the security of America.[4] From the CAIR Web site, one would gather that America was the problem, not rogue Islamists. The recent arrest of Abdurrahman Alamoudi—the founder of the other major national organization, American Muslim Council—has exposed him as an agent of the Libyan government. He has allegedly been using the American Muslim community's goodwill to advance the interests of Mu'ammar Qadaffi's Libya.[5]

Even the more progressive Los Angeles–based Muslim Public Affairs Council (MPAC) has very little to offer in terms of a strategy for fighting terrorism or anti-Americanism in its various forms. In an eighty-page position paper on counterterrorism, MPAC is more critical of the Department of Justice and

3. See Muqtedar Khan, "Putting the American in 'American Muslims,'" *New York Times*, September 7, 2001. Also see Jane Lampman, "Muslim in America," *Christian Science Monitor*, January 10, 2002.

4. See Council on American Islamic Relations, http://www.cair-net.org.

5. For details about Alamoudi's arrest and his connections to the Libyan government, see the brief filed against him in a Virginia court by U.S. Immigration and Customs Enforcement (http://news.findlaw.com/hdocs/docs/terrorism/usalamoudi93003cmp.pdf).

the U.S. government than it is of al Qaeda, Hamas, or any other rogue Islamist groups.[6] MPAC even includes an apologia for Wahhabism, but has no advice on how the United States should deal with the fact that fifteen of the nineteen attackers on September 11 were from Saudi Arabia. MPAC's recommendations are designed to make life easier for American Muslims (an understandable and important objective) and to advance Palestinian interests as necessary for American security (once again, revealing greater concern for the Arab world than for America itself). Indeed, the paper does not have anything substantive to say about al Qaeda or about how to deal with it and its sympathizers overseas and at home. But MPAC does deserve credit for at least trying to do the right thing. The limitations of its paper are merely reflective of a lack of policy expertise.

As long as these organizations are seen as being truly representative of American Muslims, American Muslims cannot be a useful ally in America's war on terrorism. Before that can happen, there must be a two-pronged regime change within the American Muslim community. First, those leaders who have used American Muslims to advance Arab interests must be marginalized. Second, American Muslim priorities must change. American Muslims must become a community for themselves and cease to be an instrument of the Muslim world. When American Muslim leaders and the American Muslim community begin to work in their own true self-interest, only then will they be able to assist America in fighting terrorism and other forms of anti-Americanism.

It is, however, important to note that, as early as December

6. See MPAC's position paper on terrorism, "A Review of US Counterterrorism Policy: American Muslim Critique and Recommendations," http://www.mpac.org/bucket_downloads/CTPaper.pdf.

2001, Imad ad-Deen Ahmad, a one-man think tank who is a libertarian and a dedicated Muslim, wrote a powerful article in which he argued that it was the Islamic duty of Muslims to bring the criminals responsible for September 11 to justice.[7] In that well-argued paper, Ahmad exhorts Muslims in general, and American Muslims in particular, to go beyond words and let their actions against bin Laden speak as their condemnation of his actions and his organization. It is amazing that Mr. Ahmad is not sought out by the National Security Council or the Department of Homeland Security. The global strategies he has proposed for dealing with al Qaeda are far better than any that the Bush administration has so far come up with. It is a pity that Muslim organizations and the Bush administration have not acted on his suggestions.

Ahmad makes several important points, the most important of which is his compelling moral argument that all Muslims, and especially American Muslims, are duty bound to bring the terrorists who perpetrated the attacks of September 11 to justice. He clearly indicates that it is not enough that Muslims unequivocally condemn the acts; they also must act, collectively and decisively, in pursuit of justice. Ahmad is also critical of the conspiracy theories that are circulating in the Muslim world, and he shows how these false claims are contrary to Islamic values. Ahmad identifies various projects that Muslim NGOs and international governmental organizations, such as the Organization of the Islamic Conference, can undertake to arrest the tide of extremism, delegitimize terrorism, and indeed launch, in his words, "a jihad against terror."

---

7. See Imad ad-Deen Ahmad, "Islam Demands a Muslim Response to the Terror of September 11," *Middle East Affairs Journal* 7, no. 2–3 (Summer–Fall 2002).

George W. Bush Alienates American Muslims

American Muslim organizations have not made all the mistakes, however. Several misconceived policies of the Bush administration have deprived it of valuable assistance that American Muslims could provide in the war on terrorism. The administration, in its characteristically arrogant and short-sighted way, insulted and alienated the United Nations; then, when the United States needed the United Nations, the latter was unwilling to cooperate. Similarly, the Bush administration has mistreated and alienated the American Muslim community, which once voted for him overwhelmingly but which is now determined to see his back.

Most American Muslims feel that by passing the U.S. Patriot Act, which they think undermines their freedoms, and by invading Iraq even though there was no credible intelligence about its unconventional weapons programs and the supposed linkage between Saddam Hussein and al Qaeda, Bush has betrayed their trust. They feel that he is now guided by the prejudice of supposed Islamophobes, such as Daniel Pipes, Jerry Falwell, and Pat Robertson, who are determined to roll back the growth of Islam in America. President Bush's insistence on getting Daniel Pipes on the board of the U.S. Institute of Peace, by hook or by crook—appointing him when Congress was in recess—has convinced Muslims that Bush will go to inordinate lengths just to insult the American Muslim community.

In addition, President Bush's steadfast support for Israel, no matter what it does, and his misadventure in Iraq strengthen the perception that there is a war on Islam and make many American Muslims less willing to do anything to assist America at this moment. Muslims are not going to help America if America is seen as using September 11 to help

Israel. Perhaps, if there were a new administration in Washington, American Muslims might be more willing to come forward and work with the American government.

What Role Can American Muslims Play in the War on Terrorism?

American Muslims have an enormous potential to become an important ally in America's war against extremism. If consulted and brought into counterterrorism planning, they can help America become more effective, more focused, and more cost effective. Four areas of assistance stand out.

First, with regard to threat assessments and threat identification, American Muslims could have provided the Bush administration with a more accurate picture of the potential for threats from within the United States. Their analysis would have helped make the Department of Homeland Security a smaller, more effective, and less expensive institution. The American government is unnecessarily spending vast amounts of resources in surveillance of groups and individuals who do not constitute a threat, while they may be overlooking those who could be problematic. American Muslim input on this subject could be immensely useful.

Many U.S. policy makers continue to err in understanding and predicting the behavior of Muslim groups; the postwar chaos in Iraq is a case in point. If American Muslims had been more involved in the management of Iraq after the war, it would have been easier for Washington to establish better communications and perhaps gain more cooperation from various groups within Iraq.

Second, American Muslims could have given a Muslim face to America's response to September 11. That option, had it been pursued, could have averted the feeling in much of the

Muslim world that the war on terrorism is a Christian-Zionist crusade against Islam. The Bush administration erred by not appointing a Muslim to a high position at the Department of Homeland Security. Senator Spencer Abraham—an American Christian proud of his Arab heritage, and a trusted Republican—might better serve the country there than at the Department of Energy.

Similarly, the Bush administration should have appointed a number of prominent American Muslim athletes, such as Hakeem Olajuwon, and some imams, such as Imam Hamza Yusuf (an American convert to Islam who is well respected in the Muslim world), as special goodwill envoys to the Muslim world. The State Department is now attempting this in a less prominent way—better late than never. A more prominent Muslim presence in America's diplomatic and counterterrorism endeavors would have gone a long way, not only in preempting the rise of anti-Americanism but also in building trust between America and the Muslim world.

Third, there is the deficit in human intelligence. Some important assets that American Muslims can bring to the war on terrorism include human intelligence, cultural insights, linguistic skills, and experience and awareness of the diversity within Islamic groups and movements. It is possible that the FBI, CIA, and NSA can access these resources through recruitment, but voluntary support in this area from the community can be priceless.

Fourth is public diplomacy. Many American Muslim scholars have argued that Islam and democracy are compatible. The Bush administration could have recruited several of those scholars to make this case in Iraq and to help design Iraqi democracy and write its constitution. Without significant input from respectable Muslim scholars, the Iraqi constitution may not stand up to possible accusations that it is un-Islamic and written to make Iraq subservient to American interests.

Relatedly, an important arena where the United States badly needs its Muslim citizens is in countering anti-American propaganda. Islamists, as well as several Muslim governmental media, have launched a propaganda war against the United States in response to the war on terrorism. This anti-American media offensive is determined to focus on U.S. foreign policy excesses and failures. It also seeks to explain every aspect of American policy as if it were serving only Israeli interests. With American Muslims as spokespersons surfing the media and the airwaves in the Muslim world, the United States would have a better chance of sending out a more balanced view of its policies.

American Muslims can also counter the abuse of Islam by rogue Islamists and help to undermine their legitimacy. American Muslim scholars have consistently maintained that *hirabah* ("terrorism") is not jihad and is strictly prohibited by Islamic principles and law. They have also argued how suicide bombings violate the Islamic ethic of self-defense and are not legitimate instruments of jihad.[8] If the voice of American Muslim scholars were given more attention, say through a White House–sponsored conference on jihad, many of the moderate and liberal elements in the Muslim world would recognize the fallacies in the so-called Islamic edicts of rogue Islamists and the scholars who support and justify their cause.

Restore Balance to America's Foreign Policy

American foreign policy is currently being shaped by a small group of close-minded individuals who are open neither to

8. Sohail H. Hashmi, "Not What the Prophet Would Want: How Can Islamic Scholars Sanction Suicidal Tactics?" *Washington Post*, June 9, 2002.

criticism nor to suggestion. The White House has become a victim of groupthink. It even refuses to recognize that its foreign policy agenda is in shambles. Bin Laden is still out there, as is al Qaeda; Americans are dying nearly every day in Iraq and Afghanistan, and the American economy is bleeding constantly. Anti-Americanism has reached shocking proportions, even in countries considered to be traditional allies. The administration itself claims that serious threats to American security are still out there and that much of the world is decidedly committed to not cooperating with the United States. To put it bluntly, American foreign policy under Bush is a colossal failure and is even potentially dangerous to America's security and economic health.

This administration would do well to listen to some moderate Muslim voices in shaping its foreign policy objectives and in determining its tactics. Most American Muslims have the same vision for the Muslim world as does the Bush administration. Most American Muslims want wholesale regime changes and the establishment of democracy in the entire Muslim world. They want to see the general human rights environment improving and wish that prosperity and freedom would take root in the Muslim world. The difference is that American Muslims would recommend strategies that are more humane and that involve less bombing and killing. The Bush administration needs American Muslims, and it is time it acted on this need and included them in its policy deliberations.

At the same time, patriotic American Muslims need the administration. Muslims for America are now locked in a struggle with Muslims for the Muslim world to determine the overall purpose and direction of the community. The government must find a way to bypass the dominant Muslim organizations that are determined to advance foreign interests, and instead recruit American Muslims whose hearts are wedded to America. Doing so could tip the balance. These Muslims must be committed to Islam as well as to America, for Muslims who reject or ridicule Islam will not enjoy support within the community and cannot mobilize the goodwill of the community to help with America's crisis of legitimacy in the Muslim world. Truly, American Muslims and the U.S. government need each other.

Public
Arts

11 | Déjà Vu: The ABCs of Public Diplomacy in the Middle East

Martin Kramer

There is a good deal of talk and hand-wringing about the "hearts and minds" problem in the global war on terrorism. Even Secretary of Defense Rumsfeld has ruminated over the matter, dropping some of his famous snowflakes on his staff in asking that a better job be done with respect to the nonmilitary aspects of the challenge. Rumsfeld is rightly concerned not only with dispatching this generation's terrorists but also with short-circuiting the processes that are producing the terrorists of the future.

Secretary Rumsfeld is probably right to worry that the United States and its allies are not doing a thorough job on what the Pentagon calls the nonkinetic aspects of the war on terrorism. In some areas, such as monitoring and interrupting the flow of money to terrorist organizations, some progress has been made. But in others, such as education reform and U.S. public diplomacy, it is not clear how much has been achieved. It may even be that in the public diplomacy domain, the United States has gone backward.

But how to tell, and what to do? It is difficult to generalize from anecdotes; polls are often unreliable; and no one has yet collected, collated, and analyzed all the relevant data. All of that needs to be done. Meanwhile, however, it is possible to sketch out the basic dos and don'ts of a public diplomacy campaign, because such campaigns have been designed and implemented before—by others in the Middle East and by Americans elsewhere. So, before we get to the question of whether to go with satellite television alongside FM radio, or whether to emphasize American pop culture or America's traditions of tolerance, or whether this Gallup poll or that Zogby survey tells the real story, we have to remind ourselves, on a fundamental level, what public diplomacy has been and should be about.

Learning from France (Yes, Really)

As suggested above, the "hearts and minds" problem in the Middle East is not a new one. Every non-Muslim authority that has projected power into the Middle East has faced the problem of winning Muslim hearts and minds. This is because the projection of non-Muslim power into that part of the world has always been suspect in Muslim hearts and minds, often with good cause. Past episodes of Western public diplomacy, successful and not, offer both edification and some entertainment—and where better to begin a potted history of public diplomacy in the Middle East than in the Mediterranean Sea in 1798?

In that year, Napoleon invaded Egypt. On one of the approaching French ships, there was, of all things, an Arabic printing press. While en route, Napoleon ordered a broadsheet to be printed on that press for distribution. The points he wanted to make have an oddly familiar ring. "You will be told," read the broadsheet, "that I have come to destroy your religion; do not believe it! Reply that I have come to restore your rights, to punish the usurpers, and that more than the Mamluks, I respect God, his Prophet, and the Qur'an."

To drive home the point of his empathy for the Muslims, Napoleon added this evidence of sincerity: "Did we not destroy the Pope, who said that war should be waged against the Muslims? Did we not destroy the Knights of Malta, because those insane people thought God wanted them to wage war against the Muslims?" If Napoleon had hired speechwriters, he could not have paid them too much.

Not only were the French going to show friendship to Islam, or at least to claim it, they were also going to promote a revolutionary thing called equality. But they would do so in a way that presumed to be consistent with Islam. "All men are equal before God," said Napoleon's proclamation. "Wisdom, talents, and virtue alone make them different from one another." Here was the first stab at democracy promotion. (Of course, the French also warned that any villages that did not surrender would be burnt to the ground, but that's another matter.)

There is a good deal more in the 1798 French declaration to the Muslims, and every aspiring public diplomacy officer should master it. In this foundation statement of Western public diplomacy, diplomacy officers will find the two key talking points of any effective campaign already in mature readiness: promise to use your power to pursue enlightened ends that will benefit Muslims, and profess absolute respect for Islam.

There is a second famous instance of Western public diplomacy toward the Muslim world that deserves careful attention. During the First World War, France and Britain (and

Russia) faced a serious problem: the Ottoman sultan, who was also the Caliph of the Islamic world and, not insignificantly, an ally of Germany, issued a jihad proclamation against them. The proclamation was circulated in every Muslim language, much like an Osama bin Laden video is circulated today by other means. The sultan's proclamation pointed out, "He who summons you to this great holy war is the Caliph of your noble Prophet."

At the time, all three of the aforementioned Entente powers ruled over subject Muslim peoples in the millions, and naturally, they feared the prospect of uprisings. In response, Britain and France launched very sophisticated public diplomacy campaigns. Muslim notables were persuaded to certify that the Entente powers allowed Muslims complete freedom of religion. The British and French also made strenuous efforts to get out the word that the sultan's call to jihad was not genuine. It was, they claimed, not really the work of the Caliph but of the Young Turk regime acting at German suggestion. The proclamation, they insisted, was a fake "holy war made in Germany."

But the big coup came for the Entente powers when the British persuaded the sharif of Mecca, a descendant of the Prophet, to raise the standard of revolt against the Ottoman caliph in Mecca itself. All in all, this worked very well. The Allies had very little trouble from their Muslim subjects throughout the war. The lessons for us today should be clear: Get Muslims with the best Islamic pedigree on your side, and try to line up whoever has the say in Mecca.

In World War II, the "hearts and minds" problem returned. Indeed, the British had an even bigger problem in the 1930s and 1940s than they had had twenty years earlier. Large portions of Muslim, and especially Arab, opinion were pro-Axis. Many Arabs thought the British had betrayed promises of independence made during the previous war—perhaps because Hitler hosted the Mufti of Jerusalem in Berlin, claiming just that. The leading German orientalists were summoned to translate *Mein Kampf* into Arabic, cutting out all the parts about Semites that might offend the Arabs.

This was real trouble brewing. So the British launched yet another public diplomacy campaign, predicated on the idea that Britain had more respect for Islam than any other European power. How could they demonstrate that respect in a tangible way? Build a mosque, which is how the Regent's Park Mosque in London began—as a piece of wartime propaganda.

Lord George Ambrose Lloyd, as secretary of state for the colonies, proposed the idea when war broke out, and in 1940 Winston Churchill's war cabinet put up the money to buy the site. In 1944, King George VI officially opened the Islamic Center in Regent's Lodge. In the British archives, there is file after file of press releases, radio broadcast transcripts, flyers, and brochures about the mosque to be built in London. This was quite slick stuff, and for those tasked with similar duties today, it is well worth reviewing.

When the war ended, the urgency of the mosque project faded. Indeed, the mosque itself did not get built for another thirty years. But the plan to build it served its purpose. The lesson for a Western leader today? Get thee to a mosque. Do not just profess respect for Islam; get out and show it. A year ago, an Islamic Society of North America conference was broadcast on C-SPAN. When a speaker mentioned that Queen Elizabeth had entered a mosque recently and had taken her shoes off before doing so, the audience burst into spontaneous applause. Apparently, demonstrations of respect work.

Remedial Americans

The point from this very short history is clear: other powers have done the "hearts and minds" drill before, and done it successfully. To a considerable degree, we have been there and done that. The basic components of a public diplomacy campaign to win Muslim hearts and minds are clear enough. So, why do Americans appear to be so determined not to understand them?

The main reason is that the Cold War made it too easy for the United States, just as it came into its own as a Middle Eastern power. America's adversary for over forty years was the godless, clumsy, cumbersome and downright ugly Soviet Union. Soviet commissars ruled over Muslims directly, while the God-fearing United States did not. Those commissars busied themselves with shutting down mosques and keeping Muslims from performing the hajj. It mattered not one whit how many times the Soviets sent KGB-appointed muftis to Cairo and Damascus to say that Muslims enjoyed religious freedom under Communist rule; no one in the Arab world believed it. The Soviets could offer all sorts of enticements, from MIG jet fighters to high dams, but Moscow could never erase the stigma of its reputation for hostility to religious faith. Moreover, the Saudis were themselves zealous in leading an Islamic campaign against atheistic communism, culminating in the jihad against the Russians in Afghanistan.

As long as the United States was up against the Soviets, it did not have to spend a lot of effort burnishing America's reputation as a friend of Islam. If the enemy of thine enemy is thy friend, then the United States walked in clover in the Muslim world so long as the Soviet Union existed. In retrospect, it is clear that all that changed a decade ago when the Soviet Union folded. But it took September 11 to bring home the two truths that now compel the United States to run a serious public diplomacy campaign in the Muslim world.

The first truth is now that the United States is the only great power, everyone everywhere who has a propensity to fix blame for problems on an external power is fixing it on the United States. That propensity is endemic in the Arab and Muslim worlds; because the British, the French, and the Russians are now all in the second tier of powerful nations, all the free-floating hostility of a wounded civilization is fixing itself on the United States. America stands out all too visibly, just as the World Trade Center did; all the other powers are just so many Chrysler buildings. Whatever the Russians do in Chechnya, or the Indians do in Kashmir, or the Chinese do in Xinjiang, the United States will remain the most hated of all powers. Most Americans did not realize that before September 11; they realize it now.

The second truth is that friendly Muslim governments that used to do the public relations job for America in their general neighborhood either are not doing it any longer, or are ineffective at it. For many years, the United States relied on Saudi Arabia to provide Islamic cover. But the Saudi spell—that "protector of the holy places" halo—is beginning to wear off. The religious zeal in Saudi society remains, but the royals can no longer fire it like a missile at whatever target they choose. Instead, the royals themselves seem to have become the primary target.

The Saudis will use what is left of whatever magic charms they possess to protect themselves. To judge from the current state of things, there probably will not be much left over for America. If one were to give a title to the final chapter of a book about how the United States relied on Muslim governments to provide Islamic cover, that chapter might aptly be called "15 of the 19." The meaning of September 11, put simply and starkly, is that the United States now has no choice but to do public diplomacy for itself. The end of the Soviet Union has supplied the problem in a new shape, and the end of Saudi cover has provided the need for a new solution.

This is a sad situation, perhaps, but not one beyond saving. American public diplomacy does not have to reinvent the wheel. It should take a page or two from the successful episodes in the history of the European powers. There is plenty to learn about what those tasked with managing big empires with lots of Muslim subjects did right. There is also much to learn from their mistakes.

American officials can also learn from their own experience. The United States did very well with public diplomacy during the Cold War. The present context is different: Poles and Russians and Czechs are not the same as Iranians, Uzbeks, and Yemenis. Yet some of that experience is relevant. Add to it a dash of American can-do optimism, some of the latest gadgetry, and a serious budget, and the United States will have pretty much all it needs. Almost.

The Three Nos

So much for what the United States should have and should do. There are three things, however, that it should not have or do—things that need to be avoided at all costs. These three things must be mentioned, because even as Americans seem busy ignoring the relevant history—that of others and their own—some are making directional noises in the emerging discourse of public diplomacy that need to be squelched. If the United States goes down these roads, it will surely fail.

First, the United States must not confuse public diplomacy with policy making. This confusion comes in two forms. The less dangerous form is the argument that the best way to pursue a successful public diplomacy is simply to alter American policy to make it that much easier to sell. This argument obviously confuses ends with means. There would be no need for public diplomacy if policies were easy to sell, and, just as obviously, diplomacies that are hard to sell can still be very much the right diplomacies. The purpose of public diplomacy may be formulated in a single phrase: to persuade foreign peoples to support, accept, or at least acquiesce to policies that, at first blush, they are likely to dislike, resent, or oppose.

To achieve this goal requires working in the teeth of what marketers call sales resistance. That has to be acknowledged as a given. American foreign policy is the product of a complex process; it is the job of the public diplomacy officer not to lament the outcome of the process but to sell the end product (and to do so without dwelling on its defects when presenting it to customers). Put another way, *policy is not there to create leeway for public diplomacy; public diplomacy is there to create leeway for policy.*

As fundamental and obvious as this point is, the public diplomacy function itself can become bureaucratically entrenched, and thus entrenched it will conceive itself to have its own interests. In light of this danger, the job of the real policy makers is to give public diplomacy its reading assignment and to keep it on the same page.

Confusing public diplomacy with policy making is the less dangerous of the two, precisely because it is so obvious. The second and more dangerous confusion could arise from putting the public diplomacy apparatus too close to the decision-making apparatus. Just such a confusion has been proposed by the Council on Foreign Relations' task force on public diplomacy, which recommends creating something parallel to the National Security Council for public diplomacy. The Djerejian Report proposes something similar, in the form of a new White House office to manage and coordinate public diplomacy.

No doubt, there should be someone near the Oval Office who can tell the president that it is not a good idea to use the word crusade in dealing with anything Middle Eastern. It would also be a good thing to have the occasional estimate of how a proposed course of action might affect Arab or Muslim public opinion—although the room for error in such assessments is enormous. But it is simply dangerous to put public diplomacy considerations too close to the policy-formulating machinery, because public diplomacy could then become a virtual interest group representing foreign opinion. Although that is the legitimate role of foreign embassies, the State Department's foreign contacts, and perhaps some of the ethnic lobbies that line K Street, putting public diplomacy smack in the middle of the Old Executive Office Building is to overprivilege foreign opinion in policy making, which is not the best idea in a democracy.

The second path to be avoided is this: Do not turn public diplomacy into an instrument for the domestic promotion of the multicultural ideal. In the United States, there has been a manifest temptation to do this, and it is a truly terrible idea. Arabs who live in Tunis or Damascus do not need to be convinced that Muslims in the United States can live happy and fulfilling lives as Muslims; they already know that. Anyway, it has nothing to do with promoting U.S. policy goals in the region.

The kind of distortion to which the multicultural idea gives rise has already twisted some aspects of homeland security. Anyone who has flown across an ocean on an airplane recently knows that certain "security" procedures are really rituals meant to affirm the multicultural ideal that we are all as one—and thus, we are all equally likely to be terrorists. This is nonsense, but the same potential exists in public diplomacy, which could too easily end up being an affirmative action or empowerment program for Arab-Americans. This may or may not be an end worth pursuing, but even if it is, public diplomacy is not the place to pursue it.

Public diplomacy, like homeland security, should be about getting the job done. If it can appease the gods of multicultural diversity along the way, fine—but that is not its main objective. If doing so *becomes* a primary objective, such concern for diversity will invariably produce a message that is muddled by diverse messengers. The United States needs to put out a message that is clear and unambiguous. The American ritual of presenting every possible perspective—in this case, to Arabs and Muslims in the Middle East—will leave friends isolated and bewildered and enemies dangerously confused. To the extent that the U.S. government has been guilty of such error in the past three years accounts for the counterproductive consequences of public diplomacy efforts thus far.

The third situation to avoid is an inverted structure for public diplomacy that would have Americans listening to Middle Easterners as much as or more than persuading them. This danger is implicit in the name "public diplomacy," for what is diplomacy if not a process of give and take that ultimately ends in compromise?

This belief is a popular error. The Council on Foreign Relations study, mentioned earlier, recommends "listening tours" for special panels, for example. Of course listening is important, but there is already an apparatus—American embassies and intelligence organizations—in place for that. If public diplomacy simply adds one more layer of reportage about foreign opinion, then it will have been a wasted opportunity. The point is to get the message out—to make the *other* guy listen.

Getting that message out is probably the most difficult aspect for public diplomacy to insure, because "dialogue" and "exchange" and "people-to-people" are all parts of the lexicon of public diplomacy. But one of the lessons of September 11 is that there has been too much "people-to-people"—including very free movement of people—and not enough direct persuading. The United States is not going to win hearts and minds by listening to someone complain about America and then giving him a visa.

Unfortunately, some of the initiatives now under consideration in U.S. government circles do not seem to amount to much more than that. The mere experience of America is insufficient to inoculate against anti-Americanism—we know this from numerous cases, from Sayyid Qutb to Muhammad Atta. The only possible inoculation is a steady and relentless irradiation of the Arab and Muslim worlds by a unified message, and every muscle and sinew of public diplomacy should be devoted to just that.

Road Work Ahead

At the end of the day, it may well be that public diplomacy will not make the United States loved and admired. No matter. It is no less important, and perhaps more important, that the United States be feared and respected. Indeed, no amount of explanatory verbiage emanating from Washington can substitute for the sure knowledge that the United States will defend its interests with vigor, regardless of what anyone thinks. So let us not have exaggerated expectations of public diplomacy. Public diplomacy can magnify the effect of a victory, but it cannot mitigate the effect of a defeat. In a war, even a somewhat unusual one, it is no substitute for winning.

Just ask Napoleon.

12 | Fixing Public Diplomacy for Arab and Muslim Audiences

William A. Rugh

The phrase "American public diplomacy" means, as it has meant for decades, U.S. government programs intended to support our national interests by providing information and interpretation to foreign audiences about matters relating to the United States. Unlike traditional diplomacy, which is essentially confined to intergovernmental relations, the target audience of public diplomacy is primarily nongovernmental foreign opinion leaders in the media, academia, and elsewhere.

For more than forty years, from 1958 to 1999, the primary responsibility for American public diplomacy was lodged in the U.S. Information Agency (USIA). In 1999, President Clinton decided to transfer this responsibility to the U.S. Department of State. It is true that many other government agencies, as well as many private organizations and individuals, have an impact on American public diplomacy programs when foreign audiences become aware of American actions and opinions reported in the public domain. In these days of expanding international media technology and volume, it is fair to say that the percentage of nongovernmental communications that affect the conduct of public diplomacy is growing. Nonetheless, the management of public diplomacy is strictly the State Department's responsibility, and the fact that State Department views are known to express U.S. government policy makes those views more significant than nearly all other sources of American opinion and interpretation available to foreign audiences.

The New Problem of Public Diplomacy

How should America's public diplomacy problem with Arabs in particular and the Muslim world as a whole be defined? The most urgent question for Americans today is a very specific one: How can significant Arab and Muslim support for, or acquiescence to, terrorism be counteracted? Looked at closely, that support is of a relatively narrow sort.

Recent polls show that the overwhelming majority of Arab opinion of the United States is positive toward American values and essentially all aspects of American culture and society—with the sole exception of American foreign policy. Most Arabs admire American society and U.S. leadership in science, technology, and economics. Many who are able to do so want to send their children to American universities. But Arabs are invariably critical of U.S. foreign policy, and nearly all Muslims tend to share similar views about U.S. foreign policy.[1]

Arab and Muslim criticism of U.S. foreign policy has

1. Polls reported by James J. Zogby, "What Arabs Think," Zogby International (September 2002), and Shibley Telhami, *The Stakes* (Boulder: Westview, 2002), 46–49.

increased over the past half century, and particularly in recent years. The reasons seem fairly obvious. American involvement in the Middle East was minimal before World War II, when that involvement was confined primarily to work by educators and oilmen who, in general, were regarded as bringing benefits to the region. Strong Arab nationalist sentiment in the 1950s and 1960s increasingly focused negative attention on American support for Israel, as Arabs believed that Washington was unfairly taking the wrong side in the Arab-Israeli dispute. Most Arabs and Muslims, however, continued to respect most aspects of American society and culture. Also, since pious Muslims believed communism to be a threat to Islam, America's stance against communism tended to reinforce positive attitudes toward the United States.

Since September 11, criticism of American policy has steadily increased. For the majority of Arabs and Muslims, the immediate reaction to the September 11 attack was sympathy for Americans as victims. The Arab world tended to understand the U.S. military invasion of Afghanistan and the elimination of the Taliban regime as an act of legitimate self-defense. They also regarded President Bush's initial declaration of war against terrorism as justified. As the president expanded the definition of "the enemy" beyond al Qaeda, Arabs and Muslims concluded that Bush's perception of the problem, and of the enemy, differed substantially from theirs.

Washington issued a list of terrorist organizations that was limited to Arab and Muslim groups, including, for example, Hizballah, an organization that is considered a legitimate political party in Lebanon with representatives in parliament. President Bush declared that any state not fighting terrorism was as bad as the terrorists themselves, and when American commentators writing in the press blamed Saudi Arabia and Egypt for not doing enough to counter terrorism, Saudis and Egyptians felt unfairly criticized. They replied that they had been combating terrorism for years before September 11, detaining or deporting terrorists acting against their governments. Also, as the violence between Palestinians and Israelis continued, it seemed to Arabs and Muslims that President Bush was unfairly siding with Israel and blaming only the Palestinians. Some argued and more believed that Israeli prime minister Ariel Sharon had hijacked Bush's war on terrorism for his own purposes. President Bush's subsequent linking of Iran and Iraq with North Korea as an "axis of evil" also ran counter to the trend that had developed in the Arab world to effect reconciliation with Iran and Iraq.

Washington's confrontation with Iraq, followed by the coalition's invasion, was widely opposed by Arabs and Muslims, because they did not regard Iraq as a threat to them and because they resented outside intervention. Moreover, the war seemed to them further evidence of American hostility toward Arabs and Islam, and of a dangerous willingness to use force over the objections of others. Their satisfaction in seeing Saddam Hussein toppled was undercut by increased feelings of humiliation and weakness against the lone superpower acting without soliciting or caring about their views. Unlike 1991, when the first President Bush had support from most of the Arab and Muslim world in ending the Iraqi occupation of Kuwait, President George W. Bush was widely seen as imposing a new occupation on Iraq for parochial U.S. interests.

All of these American policy behaviors seem to most Arabs and Muslims to be anti-Muslim, despite the fact that President Bush, from time to time, has said he respects Islam and has repeatedly denied that the war on terrorism is either a clash of civilizations or a war against Islam. But post–September 11 American security measures having to do with visa procedures, as well as comments critical of Islam by people like Jerry Falwell, Frank Graham, and the occasional U.S. Army officer—comments immediately conveyed to audiences abroad by CNN, Fox, and foreign media—have reinforced the impression among Arabs and Muslims that the American government and its people have turned hostile. Since September 11, the gap between the Arab perception of the world and that of Washington has steadily increased, leading to an unprecedented level of tension between the two sides.

President Bush's endorsement after the Iraq War of a new "road map" for Arab-Israeli peace was welcomed by many Arabs as a sign of American interest in helping resolve the Arab's self-declared highest-priority issue. The welcome, however, was tempered by deep skepticism that the president possessed neither the evenhandedness nor the resolve necessary to broker a settlement, mainly because, up to that point, his policies on many issues had severely undermined American credibility in the eyes of most Arabs and Muslims.

Who Is the Target of Public Diplomacy?

With all this as background, we can see that the highest-priority problem for the United States is, for the most part, restricted to foreign policy issues. Fanatical Islamists aside, most Arabs and Muslims do not hate America for what it is; they dislike America for what they think it does.

Beyond that, however, it is useful, for practical purposes, to regard Arab opinion as divided into three broad categories: friends who know us, enemies who sometimes know us and sometimes don't, and a vast middle of those who mostly don't care.

On one end of the spectrum are people who have spent time in the United States, as students or on business, and who have a reasonably sophisticated understanding of America. These are people who know some or a lot of English, who have had access to American culture and its information environment, and who tend to be the most favorably disposed to this country. They have informed, moderate, and basically positive opinions of the United States, although they too have been critical of aspects of our foreign policy. They have given us the benefit of the doubt and even defended America in discussion with their compatriots.

At the opposite extreme is a small group of radicals who are highly critical of the United States, based primarily on fear and apprehension that American involvement in their part of the world threatens their culture. Most of these radicals know little of America and have never been to America. Some, however, have been radicalized by their experience in the West—in Europe and the United States. The majority of these radicals are literate, reasonably well-educated people by standards of the region. As a rule, they are not from poor families nor from families near the bottom of their local social hierarchy.

Arab radicals have opposed existing Arab regimes as well as the United States, and the extremists among them have tended to support the use of violence and terrorism for political ends. Although these radicals have been doing this for a long time, in earlier decades they were essentially secular and leftist in orientation. But since the 1980s, they have tended increasingly to use, and presumably believe in, an Islamic fundamentalist vocabulary.

The third group is a large silent majority that tends not to focus on America very much, unless events in the region, such as the Palestinian uprising or the Iraq War, bring America to the group's inescapable attention. Members of this group come from the lower rungs of society for the most part, where considerable percentages of people—more than half in

Egypt—are either literally or functionally illiterate when it comes to political matters.

Since September 11, developments have tended to strengthen the radical group and to weaken the pro-American group. The members of the latter group have generally stopped speaking up in defense of the United States because public opinion has become so hostile. At the same time, recent events have raised the consciousness of the silent majority in ways unhelpful to American interests. Support for active opposition to America, and for terrorism, has increased among the radical minority, and others in the remaining two categories have become more reluctant to speak out against that support.

It is tempting to dismiss third world public opinion as irrelevant, and many do just that. But public opinion matters everywhere. Even rulers in authoritarian states pay careful attention to it. This is truer than ever since the growth of satellite television has eroded government controls over the information and opinion available to citizens. In the Arab world in particular, Arab satellite television that developed during the 1990s has amplified Arab voices throughout the Middle East, where local government-owned and Western media had previously dominated the discussion of international events.

It is also tempting to conclude that the only way to undermine foreign support for terrorism and to close the attitudinal gap between Washington and public opinion in the Arab and Muslim worlds would be for Washington to change its policies. Obviously, we should not change or abandon well-considered policies just because others abroad may not like them—whether because they misunderstand those policies (as is often the case in the Middle East) or because their interests genuinely conflict with our own. If that were to happen, public diplomacy would become a decidedly secondary concern.

An additional problem is that President Bush, by his policies, has badly eroded American credibility abroad, causing foreign audiences to doubt his intentions. If his administration can lead a transformation of Iraq and Afghanistan into internationally recognized successes, and if it can bring about a stable resolution to the Arab-Israeli conflict, Arab and Muslim opinion would become more favorable. But the Arab world strongly doubts that he will succeed at any of this.

Yet even in lieu of foreign policy shifts or eventual policy successes, foreign opinion can be affected by a substantial public diplomacy effort that is well planned, systematic, and well targeted. In terms of the three groups here described, it is probably futile to try to convert the few extremists away from their anti-Americanism. It is possible, however, to work with and embolden those with pro-American views and, hence, to influence the great middle of Arab and Muslim opinion, which, thanks to new technologies, is gradually being brought into the public realm.

Tools of Public Diplomacy

Decades of experience demonstrate that an effective public diplomacy program that efficiently provides relevant information about the United States and its policies must have a well-defined target audience, clear priorities for its substantive content, the most effective instruments and communication tools, and a structure of responsibility that ensures coordination. Let us briefly review these criteria as they pertain to the problem at hand.

First, as noted, the target audience should include two of the three groups mentioned above: the silent majority and friendly moderates who know and appreciate America and its values. Because it is impractical to reach all the members of those two groups, the major effort should be directed at each group's opinion leaders who are influential in their own societies today or who will be in the near future. The American effort should not try to directly target radical groups that are hostile to our values. We should leave that to others *within* the Arab and Muslim community, as they have a far better chance of effectively reaching the radicals than we do. For example, a moderate Muslim cleric with a following in his community should be a high-priority target because he can help deal with radicals and would-be radicals in terms that they understand. When appealing to moderate clerics, an important part of the message should be that it is in their own interest to keep radicals from controlling the agenda and the public discussion in their countries.

American public diplomacy priorities need to be based on an analysis of the major issues affecting Arab and Muslim opinion about America. Under current circumstances this means the highest priority should be given to explaining U.S. foreign policy and encouraging sympathetic understanding of it, because foreign policy is by far the most important source of criticism and misunderstanding of the United States today. In this context, it is important to note that although the foreign policies of the George W. Bush administration have been severely criticized abroad, they have enjoyed the support of large majorities of the American public and Congress. This huge disconnect between American and foreign opinion opens the door for the central function of public diplomacy to be activated, namely, to help explain to foreign audiences how Americans are thinking and why they support U.S. foreign policy. Arab and Muslim audiences should be told that the majority of American *society* supports U.S. foreign policies that

Arabs and Muslims oppose. The hope is that this will help open the Arab and Muslim community to new information and interpretation.

The second priority after foreign policy should be to provide information about basic characteristics of American society that are important for Arab and Muslim audiences to know and understand. In today's world, most of these audiences have access to large amounts of information about America through various channels. Indeed, at a basic informational level, they generally know much more about us than all but a tiny minority of Americans know about Arabs and Muslims.

Nevertheless, most Arabs and Muslims have important gaps in their knowledge of America—especially in terms of American government and politics. They may know from the media about our popular culture, and they may hear public statements by prominent personalities, but they tend to know little about our political system, such as the roles of Congress and the press, the court system, and the practical impact of the Bill of Rights. A broad program containing what USIA used to call "Americana" content is important in conveying an understanding of our foreign policy.

Recent American public diplomacy efforts, led until March 2003 by undersecretary of state Charlotte Beers, tended to give highest priority to Americana issues rather than to foreign policy. This is because policy under Beers focused primarily on those radical groups that hate American society and its values. Thus, considerable sums were spent on a film project showing how well Muslims were treated in America. This policy focused on the wrong target audience (the radicals), however, and did not sufficiently address the key foreign policy complaints that important audiences were expressing.

Before Beers' tenure, the Clinton administration gave

insufficient attention to foreign policy advocacy—for example, on the question of our confrontation with Saddam Hussein during the 1990s. Arab opinion increasingly criticized the UN embargo as hurting only Iraqi citizens. The U.S. government did not aggressively make public the case for continuing our policy by showing how the sanctions policy was caused by the Iraqi government's behavior. We did not explain how that policy was being manipulated to harm those segments of Iraqi society that the Iraqi regime held to be potential dangers.

Experience shows that the key to effective public diplomacy is people. There should be a cadre of professionals in our diplomatic missions abroad who are experienced in techniques of policy advocacy and Americana explication, and who are in direct contact with our target audiences. In the Muslim and Arab worlds especially, the most effective way to influence opinions and convey information is in face-to-face dialogue. Edward R. Murrow famously said that in public diplomacy, "It is the last three feet that count." Other U.S. officials abroad, including U.S. ambassadors, are also in a position to carry out public diplomacy functions when they interact with media editors, academics, and other opinion leaders.

Unfortunately, the large budget cuts for public diplomacy after the end of the Cold War, followed by the 1999 merger of USIA into the State Department, have severely reduced the number of public diplomacy specialists and undercut effective coordination between Washington and U.S. embassies abroad. The budget fell in real terms by 21 percent from 1988 to 1998. The budget has increased slightly since September 11, but it is nowhere near earlier levels. As the Djerejian Report on public diplomacy emphasized, there is an absurdly low level of support for such a critical function.

The merger of USIA into the State Department has weakened the public diplomacy function rather than strengthening it, as advocates had promised. Officers with experience in public diplomacy have less influence now and less control over programs, and public diplomacy positions are frequently filled with nonspecialists. In addition to the decline in funding, professionalism and cohesion have declined drastically. After the departure of Beers, the undersecretary for public diplomacy position was left vacant for nearly nine months—all during the recent war in Iraq and its daunting aftermath. Then Beers' replacement, Margaret Tutweiler, left the job after only a few months. The combination of resource scarcity and organizational weakness has been very harmful to the recent public diplomacy effort, at a time when that effort is needed more than ever.

The dual techniques of listening carefully to foreign opinion and engaging in dialogue are essential. For persuasion and conveying understanding, dialogue is a more powerful tool than monologue. Listening carefully to foreign opinion has the added benefit of showing respect for foreign concerns, a posture that, in itself, is likely to encourage a more rational dialogue and more moderate views. A public diplomacy professional must know what foreign audiences are thinking in matters relating to the United States. Monitoring editorials and headlines in foreign media and engaging in private discussions with key members of the foreign audience are absolutely necessary for understanding the depth of feelings and of matters that may not be clearly expressed in public forums. Most Americans would be surprised to learn how little attention U.S. policy makers pay to foreign media and that what is monitored is not systematically analyzed.

This is especially true of our efforts in the Muslim world. There is no adequate budget for it nor are there enough linguists to do this essential task. Similarly, Voice of America (VOA) call-in programs with American officials can deal effectively with foreign concerns, but these have been cut back since the 1999 merger.

Senior officials in Washington, starting with the president himself, have a significant impact on public diplomacy every time they make public statements. Yet very often, Washington officials speaking publicly are thinking about an American audience rather than a foreign one. In today's world of heavy media coverage and instant reporting, it is impossible, and unwise, to imagine that senior officials can speak only to a domestic audience. The daily briefings given at the White House and at the Departments of State and Defense are exchanges almost exclusively with American journalists asking questions that are on the minds of Americans. Rarely are the journalists sensitive to foreign opinions and concerns.

The president and other senior officials, including State Department and Pentagon briefers, must be kept aware of major issues that arise in foreign public opinion so that they can address any important misunderstandings or distortions that affect American interests. They need public diplomacy professionals to monitor and analyze foreign opinion and to report their findings so foreign opinion will be taken into account when policy decisions and statements are made. Sometimes this happens, notably when a particularly egregious mistake is made. For example, after President Bush referred to his war on terrorism as a "crusade," he was told that word was counterproductive for foreign audiences, so he did not repeat it. But Muslims remember, and it would be better had such a mistake not been made in the first place. For that, however, senior officials must be cognizant of the public diplomacy role they invariably play, and well-trained public diplomacy professionals must be there, in adequate numbers and properly placed, to do their work.

Finally, public diplomacy professionals must have an array

of communication tools that they can use to carry out their responsibilities. The following paragraphs cover the most important tools for the current circumstances.

A well-designed exchange-of-persons program can be a powerful support for American public diplomacy, again because face-to-face encounters have proven to be the most effective. Scholarships, such as Fulbrights and others, that make it possible for Arab and Muslim students, scholars, and others to come to the United States are extremely valuable means to educate those audiences about all aspects of America. Such programs do not always produce friends, of course. But they produce far more friends than avowed enemies, and knowledgeable critics are usually easier to deal with than ignorant ones.

Similarly, Americans sent abroad to study or lecture can be very helpful. The participants must be carefully chosen to ensure that they are fair-minded. It has been the wise practice not to tell American scholars what to say and for them to tolerate a certain amount of criticism of America because that usually enhances their credibility and effectiveness. Also, Arab Americans and American Muslims can often explain America abroad most effectively, just as the late Alistair Cook used to explain America on the BBC to British audiences.

Accurate, up-to-date, factual information about U.S. policy and developments in American society and culture is also essential to public diplomacy professionals. They must have information if they are to present it effectively to foreign audiences. Accuracy and truthfulness are keys to maintaining credibility in public diplomacy.[2] Officers at embassies abroad depend on daily transmissions from Washington containing

---

2. In contrast, "propaganda" is usually defined as advocacy that can use lies and distortions and that need not be attributed.

texts of U.S. statements, policy guidance messages, excerpts from American media, and reports on developments in the United States. They pass this information to target audiences based on current audience interests, drawing special attention to materials that are helpful.

Publications written for Arab and Muslim audiences can also be helpful tools, especially if they are in local languages. There used to be many such publications, but Congress cut the public diplomacy budget after the Cold War so that most were forced to go out of print. The State Department has revived the idea of magazines in Arabic aimed at Arab readers, which is a most welcome development.

The Voice of America, too, is an important public diplomacy tool because its programs are specifically designed for foreign audiences. Unfortunately, two recent developments have weakened its impact. For many years, VOA was required to follow State Department policy guidance, but under the Clinton administration, this link was broken so that VOA no longer functions in coordination with the government's public diplomacy professionals. This was a mistake; it should be fixed.

Then in 2002, the VOA Arabic service, which for decades had carried extensive policy-relevant and Americana material to a wide range of Arab audiences, was replaced by Radio Sawa, which mostly plays music for young people, severely reducing the effectiveness of our broadcasting in public diplomacy terms. Although Radio Sawa may be useful in some ways, it does not replace more serious broadcasts. There is no reason that we should be limited to sponsoring only one radio broadcast in Arabic. Radio stations are inexpensive, all things considered, especially when compared with the cost of fighter aircraft or tanks.

Gaining access to foreign media for helpful American

material and for interviews with U.S. officials has also proven to be a vital means for reaching the largest numbers of target audience members with the greatest credibility and impact. Again, personal contact with the editors of foreign media is often what persuades them to carry materials and commentaries helpful to understanding the United States. Rather than boycotting al-Jazeera and other Arab media because they carry hostile attacks on the United States, we should seek more access to them. Secretary of State Powell was wise to appear on al-Jazeera; however, very blunt, if private, pressure on the Qatari government to exercise more control over al-Jazeera may be less wise. The U.S. government should not be insisting that other governments censor their media, particularly not in the midst of a campaign to advance democracy in the Arab world.

Several other tools have also proven useful in the past and should be sharpened. One involves overseas libraries and book translations, as suggested in the Djerejian Report. Because these programs take a great deal of time and only pay off in the longer run, however, they should currently be given lower priority due to the urgency of closing the gap with the Arab and Muslim worlds.

Finally, as suggested previously, public diplomacy must have the appropriate organization and adequate funding to be effective. After the end of the Cold War, funding for American public diplomacy declined too fast and too far. This was a terrible mistake. Spending cuts mandated by Congress have reduced the number of public diplomacy professionals working abroad, reduced educational exchange programs, closed libraries, canceled vernacular language magazines, and hampered other efforts. This did not have to happen. The 1999 merger of USIA into the State Department fragmented public diplomacy and undermined it as a profession. The merger did not have to have those consequences, but it did. The coherence and professionalism of the public diplomacy function should be restored, if not by recreating USIA, then by elevating and consolidating it within the State Department. For the future of American foreign policy, it is urgent that we use proven techniques and that we find a better coordinated system and increased funding for public diplomacy for Arab and Muslim audiences.

13 | A Civilized Way to Fight Terror

Daoud Kuttab

It might seem like a contradiction to pose the question of how the United States can deal with international terror in a civilized way, but there are many nonviolent things that can be done short of, or alongside, violent responses. To understand what these might be, we must first recognize the nature of the main actor: the United States.

America the Exceptional

In a unipolar world, in which the United States has lone superpower status on the political, financial, and military levels, much more is expected of America than of any other country. As the world leader, the United States has both a kind of authority as well as a level of responsibility toward the rest of the world that no other actor has. Consequently, U.S. actions, and nonactions, carry much more weight than the actions of other countries. The country's leading status makes everything it does shine brighter than do actions of other countries and sets such actions as reference points, especially for countries in the third world that look up to the United States, even as they criticize it from time to time.

In short, America is exceptional; hence, its words have exceptional impact. What America says or even hints at has wide-ranging effects the world over. This means that with the information age in which we are living, the United States can no longer hide from the rest of the world what it says and does in America. As a result of twenty-four-hour live television, beamed nearly everywhere, every utterance of the U.S. president, his spokespersons, or people in his cabinet and his party can be heard, read, and analyzed within seconds. Statements can no longer be packaged only for a local or ethnic audience. Everyone can hear and read everything within the public discourse.

This consequent need for consistency is essential not only in the content of statements but also in the mood and style of their delivery. A smile, a frown, as well as noteworthy body language can often be interpreted and explained differently from what is intended. So it is not enough for U.S. officials to guard what they say; they need to take an active stance in following up and correcting, if need be, how their views are interpreted the world over.

The authority and power of the words spoken by U.S. officials carry great responsibility. This responsibility requires a greater degree of care about how words might be interpreted and what they might mean in different cultures. When President Bush used the word crusade to describe the U.S. campaign against terrorism, the word took on a life of its own. In the Arab world, the term was translated as "Christian war." The modern American usage of the word as a mere campaign was totally missing. It took some time for the correction to be made and even longer for many in the Arab and Muslim worlds to accept that what was meant was not a religious war but rather a campaign against terrorism.

Words, Values, and Double Standards

Although words are important, values are an even more important reference point. America has taken on the positive image not only of a successful, powerful, and rich country but also of a country based on great values. The United States stands for the best things people everywhere can hope for. The U.S. Constitution, the First Amendment, and the respect for individual rights are values beyond dispute virtually the world over. These are not just words on paper; for every American, these values are experienced every day in every state of the union.

Unfortunately, however, that is sometimes as far as it goes. Once outside the United States or when dealing with foreign policy, these values are often replaced with a variety of other considerations. People who have not lived in America, especially those who have been on the receiving end of certain realpolitik-oriented U.S. foreign policies, have little appreciation of what America stands for.

For years, people in the Middle East have been exposed to what seems to them a Janus-faced U.S. foreign policy. Human rights, the great Wilsonian concept of the people's right to self-determination, seems to stop when the subjects of discussion are Palestinians. But this has been the case for some years, so why is antipathy to the United States so high in the Arab world today? What has the United States done recently to trigger this unprecedented response?

Although these are important questions, the answers are not necessarily in any specific action by the United States, but rather in the fact that people around the world have much more access in real time, and in full Technicolor, to acts, events, and pronouncements of American officials regarding foreign policy issues. The spread of satellite television, for example, has meant that stories about, say, the human suffering of Palestinians living under Israeli military occupation enter the sitting rooms of hundreds of millions of people every day. When top U.S. officials defend or justify or merely look away from human rights violations in third world countries, few people can go back and think of the rosy picture of America as the defender of rights and the protector of freedoms.

When Vice President Cheney told Fox television that the United States "understands" Israel's need to assassinate top Palestinian officials, his statement was widely broadcast all over the Arab and Muslim world. To have a senior U.S. official understand the use of U.S. Apache helicopters by an ally in an offensive attack was hard to fathom. Some Arab commentators noted that even Timothy McVeigh was entitled to a trial, while in Palestine, Israeli generals are allowed to act as judge, jury, and executioner, with full support from the world's greatest champion of human rights, democracy, and the rule of law.

The double standard that is seen to be part of U.S. policy mystifies people in the Arab world. They cannot see how such policies can be based on U.S. national interests, let alone U.S. values, if these policies lead to 1.3 billion Muslims being alienated from the United States. Most people know that a country's foreign policy cannot be based solely on values, but where is the interest of the United States in such a result? This question leads many to conclude that the power of domestic groups to influence external policies that are not in the best national interest of the United States must be the explanation.

Most Arabs and Muslims cannot imagine that U.S. sympathy for Israel is based on genuine concern with Israel's security dilemma and its being an outpost of democracy in an otherwise authoritarian region. Their view of Israel has been shaped by a very different historical prism, which many assume America must share because it is so obvious to them. The result is that most Arabs and Muslims have become unsure of whether they are America's friend or foe, and they are prone to explaining U.S. policy behaviors in ways that most Americans, in turn, judge to be peculiar, if not conspiratorial, in nature.

Whatever the reasons for Arab and Muslim attitudes, the public attacks by many of America's own Arab allies against American policy in the Levant and in Iraq have not satisfied a population that daily witnesses what it defines as humiliation against fellow Arabs and Muslims. This is partly because Arab governments have proved themselves completely inept at doing anything about it.

Shortly after the terrorist attacks in New York and Washington, President Bush spoke to the American people calling what happened an attack against America's values. He ended by saying, "We go forward to defend freedom and all that is good and just in our world." For Americans living in the United States, these words sounded true and genuine. But for many around the world, these values have not been translated in U.S. foreign policy; these words were empty rhetoric.

The values that America stands for are the envy of well-informed human beings living in authoritarian countries around the world. Those who have lived in America and who have experienced that great country try their best to tell people around the world about it. They do so hoping that these values can be emulated in their own countries. Those who only see the results of American foreign policy, however, often attack such efforts by pointing to the apparent contradiction between values preached and practices observed.

In the past, the U.S. government was often able to get away with this contradiction. Although accused of not doing enough by some right-wing circles in America, friendly Arab countries would protect the U.S. image, and their government-controlled media would ensure that America's policies were defended. But globalization, which has been a main vehicle of America's recent economic and political successes, has also brought with it media instruments (Internet and satellites) that circumvent government-controlled media and allow people freer access to the reality of U.S. foreign policy. Is it possible that the very instruments of its own success now haunt America? Preaching democracy, human rights, and transparency while supporting despots around the world weakens the U.S. position tremendously.

Within international agencies, this same issue also arises. In 2000, when the U.S. delegation walked out of the UN World Conference against Racism, held in Durban, South Africa, many around the world felt that America had allowed its policy to be hijacked by a single country, and for clearly domestic reasons. A world leader like the United States is expected to have a much more tolerant attitude and to understand that being on top means that it is more likely to be criticized than others. If the United States wants to defeat terrorism, it will have to tolerate indignities it might not otherwise tolerate.

Against Hopelessness

Although terrorism has different shapes and versions, the most dangerous kind is based on religious conviction. This danger is multiplied when one's mortal life is seen as being worthless, while the eternal life promised by religious leaders seems so grand. To counter such religious zealotry, various levels of responses are needed. Proper religious education and preaching are extremely important in this case. It is also critical to provide young people with alternative examples of religious leaders who can combine spiritual knowledge with a realistic and moderate view of life and world events.

Media geared toward the community where terrorism is based are critical. What is needed is not alternative media through public diplomacy channels, because people in the region will not trust it. Instead, local, indigenous media must be influenced. Although it might be more difficult to get a message into these media outlets, any success with such media can have beneficial long-term effects. Influencing local media should not be limited to news. Drama, soap operas, game shows, and children's programs provide many opportunities that are rarely used to effect change in attitudes.

Public opinion is not restricted to media, of course. Positive role models are needed to encourage young people. For example, sports heroes and music stars can be tapped to give messages of tolerance and moderation.

After all, terrorism does not fall from the sky. It needs a fertile environment in which to develop. Terrorism is not a virtual reality but a real act that requires flesh-and-blood individuals to carry it out. A true search for the causes that drive people to act in such a violent way is a necessary first step in understanding and dealing with this threat. Such an attempt ought not be done in a heavy-handed, arrogant manner, but rather with a genuine interest in understanding those affected. Such empathy is a prerequisite to a true understanding of the underlying causes; without it, we will be unable to tackle those causes in an effective way.

Finally, to tackle these worldwide problems, one must

come down to the level of the individuals who are involved. Understanding that terrorism is the weapon of the weak and helpless is a step toward understanding what drives people to carry out such inhumane acts, even at the cost of their own lives. A psychological profile of those carrying out acts of terrorism clearly shows the extremely high level of frustration and helplessness they felt. When a person's own life becomes so worthless and when the hope of a future disappears, individuals have little care or concern for the lives of others.

Therefore, the best ways to combat terrorism are to change the atmosphere in which it grows and to replace the sense of hopelessness that so many young people experience with a vision for a better tomorrow. Naturally, lip service is not enough. People need to see that realistic and genuine visions are being followed in such a way that they can be convinced that their lives will likely improve. Public diplomacy can be an adjunct to such a process but never a substitute for it.

14 | Relating to the Muslim World: Less Is More?

Ellen Laipson

Twenty-two years ago, Ramadan fell in the middle of summer, and I was residing in Rabat, Morocco, doing research and enjoying the opportunity to live in a Muslim country of great charm and beauty. I had no formal link to the U.S. embassy. However, as a courtesy to me as a Library of Congress employee, I was allowed some office space at the U.S. cultural office, part of what was then called the U.S. Information Agency—since integrated into the Department of State.

The USIA office was in a modest downtown office building that happened to be close to the cultural office of the Union of Socialist Soviet Republics. To this day, I remember that USIA virtually shut down its programming during Ramadan, while the Soviets held a daily film program, allowing young people to spend an hour in a cool dark place off the shimmering sidewalks. The films were not memorable, to say the least. But as I sat in the Soviet cultural center, I wondered whether the access provided to these regular folk—decidedly not denizens of the embassy cocktail circuit—would make a lasting impression on their political views.

Perhaps not. But it stimulated me to reflect on whether our own ideas of outreach are too elitist and whether our tradition of respecting others' religion actually cuts us off from benign interactions with people of different faiths. In the years after my visit, the U.S. cultural office moved to the affluent suburbs for security reasons; even fewer Moroccans now have access to films, libraries, or cultural activities sponsored by the U.S. embassy. Today, too, we hear of U.S. reluctance to be visibly associated with secular or missionary schools in the Muslim world, out of fear of offending local sensibilities. In addition, many American nongovernment organizations and embassies struggle to interact in a normal way with "moderate" Islamists without running afoul of all the new antiterrorism rules and regulations.

The secretary of state, meanwhile, hosts elaborate *iftar* receptions with Muslim ambassadors, and the president has learned to send end-of-Ramadan greetings to Muslim Americans and to Muslim leaders around the world. The United States has much goodwill and good intentions to do the right thing by Muslim friends and partners, but there is clearly a lot of confusion and fumbling, too.

How do we get it right? Is it possible to be fair, open, and honest and have our message understood as transmitted? Or are our efforts to communicate officially with Muslim societies doomed to fail because our own cultural norms are so different from Islamic ones, and because of the agitated state of mind that many, if not most, Muslims have toward the United States these days?

The New Context of Public Diplomacy

I believe we have serious problems on both the sending side and the receiving side of public diplomacy. We need now to reflect carefully on how much, if any, of the critical society-to-society communication can be managed by government. In the information age, after all, it is increasingly difficult to keep different kinds of messages in distinctly separate channels. Governments have many information-related policies and strategies: there is information generated by the bureaucracy for internal deliberations on policy; there is information in the official exchanges of diplomacy and intelligence prepared to convince allies or to bully adversaries; there is occasionally information deliberately altered to influence a foreign population (psychological operations or propaganda); and then there is the regular press function, with information prepared to inform the American public and the American media about the government's policies and activities. I believe that the information revolution has made it virtually impossible to keep these channels separate. Information moves too fast, and there is much greater transparency in government operations than there used to be. The result is that a message designed for a particular audience is now instantly available to a global audience. It is no longer possible to fine-tune a message for a distant Muslim audience and not have your political rivals at home know about it. It is equally difficult to share with the American public a policy's nuances without having it dissected in salons in Cairo and Karachi.

Public diplomacy, therefore, is an anachronism in today's world, and as such, it is probably doing more harm than good. The transparency required in our own society clashes directly with the notion of manipulating perceptions and opinions. For successful manipulation to occur, you must *appear* to be doing something sincere and straightforward. But in today's world, we talk in real time about why and how our government functions; one cannot publicly acknowledge that we are "spinning" our stories without that acknowledgment having an effect on the target of the spinning.

Would it not make more sense, therefore, to expand the press and information capacity to work in a more direct and honest way in talking about our policies and, yes, their shortcomings? Couldn't our press spokesmen take on a bit of additional work, giving more background and explanation of our policies, as opposed to the highly condensed sound bites they are expected to provide? Couldn't our media be staffed by people who can retrieve, on request, additional data or background on our policies and their impact?

Public diplomacy as conceived and ridiculed during the Bush administration has been too close to the marketplace and not nearly close enough to the underlying logic of our policies. By admitting that the government was importing some Madison Avenue techniques, we revealed too much of an inclination to our own crass thinking—that policies are commodities that must appeal to the current fads of consumers. The Madison Avenue approach undermined the more noble and often contradictory struggles behind policies that may not please everyone but that nevertheless embody our national aspirations and our democratic processes.

Public diplomacy toward the Muslim world also contains many other pitfalls. Muslims in general and Arabs in particular can distinguish between American consumer goods they like and American official policies they loathe. But we act as if we are surprised that consumers of our goods don't like us after all. We have also conflated the pro-Americanism that may exist in the Muslim world, often very superficially, with support for other aspects of American culture and power. We need to understand the complex attitudes toward us in a more nuanced way. We should not try to label people in the region; it is an insult to them and to our own political culture, which professes to have high tolerance for political disagreement.

Missing the Mark

There are at least three specific respects in which our efforts to communicate with Muslim audiences from official platforms have missed the mark: economics, the pace of change, and the role of religion in public life. Let's take a quick look at each.

Economics

When we try to commoditize our foreign policy for Muslims, we show glaring insensitivity to prevailing views about economic values. In mainstream American political discourse, free elections and free markets are equally important principles. For Muslim believers, however, the allocation of resources needs to address social justice, which resembles an economic model probably closer to European social democratic party positions than to American capitalism. Muslims may be able to embrace some, even many, of the core political concepts we hold dear, but preaching capitalism to societies with already distorted markets and income distributions—and with rampant poverty—may not make sense to most Arabs. It sets us up for a policy failure.

Of course, there are many capitalists in Muslim societies who have thrived due to their entrepreneurial skills and their business acumen. They are important members of the political and social elite in Egypt, Syria, North Africa, and Pakistan. Sometimes these capitalists become advocates for economic reforms because they are more attuned to the need to adapt to new EU policies, for example, or because they see opportunities in seeking free trade agreements with the United States. But when we think about the broader malaise in the Muslim Middle East, we are often talking about the part of the population that has not benefited from the profits of the private sector. New linkages between our capitalist system and Arab economic elites would not foster greater sympathy or support for U.S. policies among the ranks of the unemployed.

If we are truly open to an agenda for change in the region, as the Bush administration has declared, then we must be in a listening mode. Demand for change in the Arab world or in the large Muslim societies of southern Asia does not even remotely mean that would-be reformers or democrats would choose the American model, which has no social safety net, underfunded retirement programs, and no universal health care. Instead, agents for change who may be our best partners on the political side may have quite different ideas about how to distribute and share a state's wealth and its foreign aid revenues. It is important that we show some flexibility and tolerance; a relentless drumbeat extolling the virtues of the Washington consensus on market economics will not serve our broader goals in the Muslim world.

Timing

We also miss each others' signals when it comes to matters of timing. Americans are impatient and want to measure attitudes of the moment. Our public diplomacy bureaucrats want to know how people in other countries are reacting to our "message" so that they can fine-tune it for the next poll, or even for the next day's news cycle. But attitudes in nondemocratic societies, where most Muslims live, are not easily changed. Cynicism from living with hypocritical rulers does not easily dissipate, as is evident in post-Saddam Iraq. The would-be democrats of the Muslim world have acquired some deeply ingrained beliefs about how the world works, and these beliefs cannot be shaken quickly with a few advertisements or articles.

We must reconcile ourselves to the fact that attitudes and behavior do not change quickly and that our efforts to manipulate or change deeply ingrained beliefs and experiences are often feckless. If attempted in culturally inappropriate ways, these efforts can do more harm than good and, in so doing, can feed the region's robust proclivity to conspiracy theories. For example, in our saturated information market, there is enormous pressure to have "news" of change in Iraq that actually misinforms world publics about how change truly does occur.

Religion in the Public Sphere

We do a poor job communicating about religion in public and about the ties between religion and state. Clearly, across the Muslim world, theologians and independent thinkers are in a fierce and important debate on this issue. There is a wide range of issues and opinions: Should clergy be employees of the state? Have Iran's clerics been given, or taken, too much authority in matters of state? How should new constitutions address religion in societies where not all citizens are Muslim?

The United States, again, cannot claim to have the answers to such questions. Americans are raised with a myth about the separation of church and state, but our behavior suggests considerable confusion on the point. We have had presidents, including George W. Bush, who are deeply religious and speak of their beliefs in ways that can alienate or offend citizens who hold different beliefs, or who do not believe the president should see his official duties as having any religious content whatsoever.

Meanwhile, the secretary of state invites Muslim diplomats to the formal diplomatic rooms at the Department of State to celebrate the breaking of the fast on Ramadan. At first glance, many are pleased, even touched, at this gesture of cultural goodwill to the world's Muslims. But such a gesture seems strange, even patronizing, as a public demonstration of respect for a religious rite. Would it not be simpler and truer to our own principles to be consistent with respect to defining religion as a private matter? All that a liberal, Lockean state needs to do is create and preserve an environment in which there is freedom of religion and tolerance for all. Wouldn't that be the most appropriate U.S. message for the Muslim world?

Other Ways to Communicate

I am not suggesting that engaging with Muslim societies is too hard or should not be a goal of U.S. policy. I am simply suggesting that "public diplomacy" is not the way to do it. If one considers the current structure of the State Department, there is an undersecretary for public diplomacy and public affairs, with three bureaus reporting to that senior official (the Charlotte Beers position, vacant for many months until filled briefly by Margaret Tutweiler). The three bureaus that report to the undersecretary run important and useful programs that permit interaction with diverse groups in Muslim societies. There are cultural and educational programs, media exchanges, training opportunities, and more. I would reallocate the funding of this part of the State Department to maximize impact on the long-haul issues, education in particular. I would phase out the more questionable public diplomacy activities that have generated controversy with no discernible benefit to the United States.

For example, our press activities should be expanded. We

should help new foreign media establish professional standards—a worthy contribution as countries even in the more closed parts of the Muslim world make the transition from government monopolies on news and information to the wider world of open information.

If we are open to changing our ways of engaging with the Muslim world in the hopes of avoiding further estrangement, we also need to grapple with the elitism of our policies. More often than not, our programs are looking for winners, trying to scout out future leaders in whom to invest. This is true across a range of overseas activities that the U.S. government supports, with the notable exception of antipoverty programs and humanitarian relief activities. In diplomatic, educational, and military exchanges, we aim high. We are looking to invest in success, in individuals who may well emerge as a next generation of leaders and decision makers.

There is nothing inherently wrong with this policy, but it may not be sufficient as a communications strategy. Given the widening gap between haves and have-nots in Muslim societies, should we not also try to reach out to the populations that are vulnerable to hatred and despair and violence? Might a different kind of U.S. engagement help prevent the spread of suicide bombers? Former U.S. peace negotiators have expressed regret for neglecting civil society in Israel and Palestine, the nonofficial populations that must minimally accept the governments' policies for those policies to succeed, even in nondemocratic places. One former negotiator, Aaron David Miller, now heads Seeds for Peace, the innovative program that brings teenagers from key conflict zones (Arab-Israel, India-Pakistan) to the United States to communicate and even form bonds of friendship. It is worth considering whether a restructuring of programming priorities from elites to a mix that includes more popular audiences, and young people in particular, might not be the strategic investment that this particular historic juncture requires.

These modest ideas remain at a level of generality and cannot adequately address the deep divide that exists between the West and segments of Muslim society in a large group of countries. Generalizations can also cause harm by failing to recognize the enormous diversity of both American and Muslim societies. In the end, it is up to individuals to build the bridges and to find ways to communicate. In an increasingly interdependent world, more business partnerships, marriages, and friendships can be formed, and we should encourage and celebrate those ties. But governments do matter because they represent, for good or ill, the idea of a nation, the aspirations of a culture and its people. Our government has labored hard, and many individuals do so with great sensitivity and skill, but we need to look very closely at our policies and our style of communicating with the Muslim world. Perhaps it's time for our government to simplify and reduce the number of information initiatives it generates toward the Muslim world and to spend more time making sure its policies are wise and grounded in fairness and principle. Then the communication piece will follow naturally.

15 | A Practical Guide to Tapping America's Underappreciated, Underutilized Anti-Islamist Allies across the Muslim World

Robert Satloff

With more than 1.3 billion Muslims worldwide, it is not realistic for the United States government—working both independently and in concert with other governments, international organizations, and private initiatives—to thoroughly "drain the swamp" in which Islamist[1] terrorist organizations find their recruits. Even if one were to accept a low-end estimate of the number of Islamists worldwide (say, 5 percent of all Muslims) and a low-end estimate of the number of terrorists or their activist sympathizers—financiers, logistical supporters, ideological advocates—among them (say, 1 percent of all Islamists), then there are at least 600,000 hard-core

1. Islamist is defined here as a Muslim who seeks—either through peaceful or violent means—the imposition of Qur'anic law (Sharia) and a Qur'anic-based state, rejecting the legitimacy of the existing political structure in his/her country or region. Although organically antidemocratic (i.e., opposed to "rule of the people"), Islamists can equally reject democratic systems and monarchical ones, the principal point of departure for them being the imperative to impose "divine law" in place of human-made systems of governance.

radicals fishing for followers in a sea of at least 60,000,000 potential recruits.[2] To identify, target, isolate, co-opt, and, in some cases, neutralize the former is a gargantuan task. To do the same to the latter is patently impossible.

If fully "draining the swamp" is not achievable, however, there remains much that can be done to decrease the number of Muslims who become Islamists and to decrease the number of Islamists who become terrorists or their activist sympathizers. Each of these challenges requires different tools and different strategies. In essence, whereas decreasing the number of Islamists who become terrorists is principally the province of intelligence and security agencies, decreasing the number of Muslims who become Islamists is a much wider concern that touches on numerous aspects of U.S. foreign policy.

Curtailing the appeal of Islamism should be a matter of prime importance to practitioners of what is popularly known as "public diplomacy." To many, public diplomacy is merely a less grating term for "public relations abroad," or the less-than-fine-art of packaging and selling America to foreign audiences. Although that is an element of the larger picture, public diplomacy is—or *ought* to be—much more than that.

Just as traditional diplomacy revolves around strengthening allies, weakening adversaries, and advancing America's interests and values, the same can be said of public diplomacy. Although the targets are different (peoples, not government) and the operational time frame is often longer, the objectives are similar: empowering friends, undermining the influence of adversaries, and nurturing popular understanding of (and, one hopes, support for) U.S. national interests and values.

2. Daniel Pipes, for example, suggests that "perhaps 10 to 15 percent" of all Muslims subscribe to "militant Islam." See Pipes, *Militant Islam Reaches America* (New York: W.W. Norton, 2002), 3.

Unfortunately, too few professional public diplomats view their mission in terms of allies and adversaries. Indeed, the fundamental problem of U.S. public diplomacy in the post–September 11 era is that it has rarely evinced a clear sense of mission, has rarely differentiated clearly between friend and foe, and has rarely focused its energies on extending a helping hand to those elements in society—especially in Muslim-majority countries—that are America's natural allies in the struggle against radical Islamism.

Defining a detailed, full-scale, soup-to-nuts program to achieve those objectives is beyond the scope of this brief essay. However, what follows are three broad suggestions that, if implemented, would begin to put U.S. public diplomacy squarely on the right side of the fight against Islamism.

Identifying and Supporting Allies

As noted above, the overwhelming majority of the world's Muslims are not Islamists. However, Islamists are often highly motivated and well funded. Although they are not choreographed by some all-knowing Islamist wizard, they coordinate well among themselves and (especially the nonviolent ones) have a sophisticated, long-range plan to advance their goals. They are people of action. In contrast, non-Islamist Muslims are defined more by who they are *not* rather than by who they *are*. They range across political and religious spectra, from radical atheists to secular, lapsed Muslims to pious, traditional, orthodox believers. They have no common program, no organizational cohesion, no way even to know who in society shares their views.

An important, and rarely pursued, step toward minimizing recruits to Islamism is to identify the potential allies among these non-Islamist Muslims, build networks of common purpose among them, and show that the United States supports them in the currency that matters in local society—that is, visibility and money.

This task requires a different sort of outreach effort than is the norm for U.S. embassies in the Muslim world. Rather than seek out "moderate Islamists" for dialogue designed to promote understanding of U.S. policies and to narrow differences over contested issues, this alternative approach would have U.S. embassies pointedly avoid contact with Islamists (except for intelligence gathering). Instead, it highlights contacts with liberal, even secular, anti-Islamist individuals and organizations. Invitations to embassy functions, participation in ambassadorial press conferences, and opportunities for exchange visits and study tours to the United States are all ways for U.S. officials to shower favor upon groups and individuals. These actions should be viewed as arrows in the larger public diplomacy quiver, for even in this era of pessimistic Pew Research Center polls of America's standing abroad, the imprimatur of the United States is sorely coveted. So are the dollars that U.S. governmental agencies and quasi-official nongovernmental organizations (like the National Endowment for Democracy's recipient agencies) dole out to local groups.

In all these programs, the guiding principle should be that the United States supports its current friends and would welcome new ones. Local political communities around the Muslim world are sophisticated: when they see that anti-Islamists of varying stripes (whether female entrepreneurs, crusading investigative journalists, or kids who win English-language spelling bees) are featured at embassy events, receive embassy grants, and win trips to the United States—with nary an Islamist among them—the message will be clear. Conversely, a clear and damaging message is transmitted when Islamists,

even of the mild variety, are the honored guests, lucky bene-
ficiaries, and welcome visitors on those events, grants, and
trips.

In addition to highlighting contact with cultural and political allies, U.S. embassies abroad and U.S. public diplomacy in
general should focus efforts on networking among groups and
individuals that, at least on the Islamist issue, share a common
approach. Like building a popular front against Nazism in
World War II or against Communism in the Cold War, this
may involve bringing together people of very different world-
views to work together for the larger cause of fighting the
spread of Islamism. Ironically, U.S. officials who either shun
"secularists" for fear of offending Muslim sensibilities, or who
have little expertise in distinguishing between traditionalist
Muslims and Islamists, are more likely to be reluctant to adopt
this approach than are local anti-Islamist Muslims themselves.
Because the latter are on the "front line," facing the rising tide
of Islamism in schools, mosques, youth groups, grassroots
organizations, and civic groups, they are more likely to take
risks. The United States should not leave such allies and
potential allies out in the cold.

Building such networks is not only important for creating
a force-multiplier of reformist activism to counter the Islamists, it is also useful for identifying individuals who could play
lead roles in specific public policy issues. Curriculum reform,
for example, is a critical battleground of the culture wars in
many Muslim societies. The traditional U.S. approach is to
offer technical assistance to ministries of education (in the
form of consultants, study trips to the United States, the professional advice of English-language officers at embassies, and
so forth). However, these efforts periodically fuel criticism and
resentment toward U.S. interference in one of the most sensitive areas of local concern.

A more effective and longer-lasting change—and one with fewer fingerprints of U.S. intervention—would result from behind-the-scenes U.S. endorsement of key reform-minded people from within the bureaucracy and civil society to positions of authority on the local and national review boards often formed to review curricula. Trying to influence the composition of various government bodies both removes the United States from direct interference in the actual process of curriculum reform and ensures that right-thinking people will be in important positions when the current battle is over and the next one is ready to be joined. This can only be achieved if U.S. embassies have already done the vital work of identifying local allies and building a communications infrastructure for networking among them.

Empowering Allies

Although lending visible political support to anti-Islamists is essential, it is not sufficient. The U.S. government should also find innovative ways to strengthen its local anti-Islamist allies. One critical, yet low-cost, arena in which the United States can empower anti-Islamists is in the information field.

One of the lesser-known phenomena in Arab and Muslim society in recent years is the flowering of nongovernmental organizations (NGOs). From remote mountainous regions in the High Atlas to the urban slums of Cairo, these organizations have sprouted up to fulfill all sorts of communal and social needs. Sometimes they emerge from the commitment of local community organizers. Sometimes they are creatures of the government, which may construct ad hoc local groups to perform special functions or fulfill services that the government chooses to channel outside the formal system. Sometimes they are local branches of organizations that have large, international followings.

Whatever their origins, tens of thousands of these organizations now exist throughout the Middle East, and a large number of them are Islamist in orientation. Many of these are registered with local governments in accordance with law, but many others operate in a legal vacuum. In a region where the central government's delivery of basic social services is notoriously bad, NGOs have emerged in many places to supply what governments either cannot or do not provide. Of course, Islamist organizations only compensate for a small fraction of what governments are not able or willing to do, but the model they offer still provides a pathway for the spread of Islamist thought and, possibly, terrorist sympathies to millions of Muslims.

Throughout Arab and Muslim countries, for example, Islamist NGOs—many financed from Saudi Arabia, some with al Qaeda links—have established powerful networks of Islamist-oriented social welfare initiatives. Following a long-term strategy of nurturing the next generation of Islamists, some of the most insidious Islamist NGOs focus exclusively on children. (Hence, for example, they might opt to fund primary schools, youth camps, and after-school programming but not current needs of the adult population, such as adult literacy programs, vocational training classes, or battered women's shelters.) Often, these NGOs operate without formal government license because their services often fill a local need. Local administrators often either look the other way or welcome these organizations, regardless of what officialdom in faraway capitals might prefer (or say they prefer).

Among anti-Islamists, even without knowing about the shadier international links of many of these groups, there is a rising sense of alarm at the spread of such Islamist social welfare activities. Many civic activists, including journalists, would take up the cudgel against the presence of these foreign-funded Islamist organizations and would be especially moved to act if they knew about the possible terrorist connections of some of these outfits. What these activists lack, however, is information, such as documentary evidence describing the political activities and funding sources of these groups and, when it exists, evidence of connection to terrorist acts and organizations. Such information is, to a large extent, part of the U.S. public record, from court transcripts, FBI documents, and congressional reports and testimonies. Indeed, the Treasury Department's Office of Foreign Asset Control publishes a list of "specially designated nationals and blocked persons" that, in the version of September 23, 2003, is 116 pages long. Many of the institutions cited on this list are the same Islamist NGOs that are active in many corners of the Muslim world.[3]

A simple, low-cost but high-value solution would be the creation of a user-friendly, Internet-based clearinghouse of information in Arabic and other local languages, outlining the operations, management, administration, financing, and personnel of all Islamist-oriented initiatives and NGOs and the linkages among them. Such an effort, if brought to the attention of the growing number of anti-Islamist activists and organizations through an aggressive, imaginative outreach campaign, would be a forceful stimulant to action. Information is power, and this sort of information would help empower anti-Islamist Muslims who are concerned about the direction of their own countries and communities to take matters into their own hands.

---

3. For the OFAC list, periodically updated, see http://www.treas.org/office/eotffc/ofac/sdn/t11sdn.pdf.

Nurturing Future Allies

In the campaign to limit the spread of Islamism, identifying, supporting, and empowering current allies is necessary but still not sufficient. To stand any chance of undercutting the Islamists' popular appeal, the United States must invest much more substantially in developing new and future allies. Here, a central battleground is children's education. Indeed, this is one area in which anti-Islamists should take their cue from Islamists, who, as noted above, have made the battle for the "hearts and minds" of young people a top priority. So far, the United States is not even putting up a fight.

In approaching this problem, it is important to remember another lesson learned from the Islamists: the power of example. In the context of populous countries like Egypt, Morocco, Algeria, and Yemen, Islamist social welfare programming is a proverbial drop in the bucket compared with what actual needs are, and even compared with what existing governments currently do. In a medium-sized town, for example, Islamists may successfully operate a model school, a professionally staffed hospital, or a well-functioning day-care center, but they cannot replace the government's massive, though admittedly broken-down, educational or health care systems. Like terrorists who have learned the ways of asymmetric warfare against conventional armies, Islamists have mastered the tools of reaping considerable public sympathy from providing *examples* of a better-run alternative system without having the responsibility or burden of actually providing such an alternative system.

Curtailing the popular appeal of Islamism should be pursued with a similar strategy. Although the U.S. government can provide some assistance to help fix local school systems, the problems are too huge—and the Islamist challenge is too urgent—to rely on that approach. Instead, Washington needs to develop alternative opportunities for anti-Islamist excellence and highly visible models of it.

Promoting English-language education should be a central focus of this effort. Knowing English does not necessarily translate into liberal thought or pro-Americanism, as the legacy of Islamist radicals from Sayyid Qutb to the September 11 bombers underscores. But English is both a portal to Anglo-American culture as well as the access route to the Internet-based information revolution. Knowing English at least gives a resident in a Muslim-majority country the opportunity to learn about America and make judgments about its policies and values without the filter of translation or reliance on biased sources of information. Indeed, studies show that access to information is not itself the key criterion in shaping views on U.S. policy; rather, it is access to different sorts and sources of information—for example, CNN versus al-Jazeera—that could be the key to determining attitudes toward the United States.[4]

Specific initiatives that could be pursued in this strategy include the following:

- Create "English-for-all" after-school programs, at no or nominal cost to parents, in cities and towns throughout the Muslim world. This should be pursued cooperatively with existing NGOs as well as with the governments of other English-speaking countries and the English Speaking Union, the British-based organization that seeks to promote the use of the English language around the globe.

4. See Matthew A. Gentzkow and Jesse M. Shapiro, "Education, Media and Anti-Americanism in the Muslim World," a study by two Harvard University students based on data from the 2002 Gallup poll of the Islamic World, http://www.people.fas.harvard.edu/~jmshapir/summary100303.pdf.

Similarly, U.S. funds should subsidize the high fees that older students are currently asked to pay for English-language training at specialized programs like AMIDEAST, thereby making those classes more accessible to a wider segment of the population. Few steps could earn the United States more goodwill in Muslim countries than to invest enough money to make English-language study free or extremely low-cost.

• Expand the existing paltry financial support for American-style educational opportunities for students of all ages throughout the Muslim world. Of the 185 U.S. government–recognized "American schools" around the world, fully one-quarter are in Muslim-majority countries and one-tenth are in Arab countries.[5] These schools—ready-made incubators of pro-Americanism—receive paltry levels of assistance from the U.S. government, only $8 million out of a combined annual operating budget of $450 million. Some schools receive as little as 1 percent of their annual operating budget from government funds. Many of these schools attract high concentrations—one-third to one-half—of local students but their often five-digit tuition fees mean that only wealthy, elite local children can attend, sometimes without regard to academic excellence. (Tuition fees for most other students are paid for by governments and international corporations.) Washington should target schools in Arab and Muslim countries for expanded merit-based, academic scholarship funds. These would help to expand the pool of local entrants and to reach beyond "old money" families to the rising middle class who yearn for a U.S.-style education and who are

5. For details on American schools around the world, see the Web site of the U.S. State Department's Office of Overseas Schools, http://www.state.gov/m/a/os/.

willing to pay substantial sums for it, but who cannot afford the exorbitant costs that cash-strapped schools are forced to charge to make ends meet.

- Support the development of U.S.-style universities throughout the Muslim world through enhanced distance-learning facilities, provision of books and supplies, educational training grants, and the like. The long-term goal should be the creation of at least one fully accredited English-language university in every country. The fact that new, U.S.-style, English-language universities are opening throughout the Muslim world—Kuwait's is the most recent, scheduled to begin instruction in September 2004—is a trend to be embraced and cultivated. Given the heightened security concerns about foreign students in the United States, combined with a financial crunch that forced a cutback in foreign Muslim and Arab students in the United States well before September 11, promoting U.S.-style universities in Muslim countries is an especially smart idea.

- Promote the distribution in Muslim countries of overstock U.S. textbooks and academic materials. Current law provides for tax breaks for book publishers to donate overstocks, but the number of books that make their way to Arab or Muslim countries is shockingly low.[6]

- Integrate the U.S. private sector, especially U.S. companies operating abroad, in English-language promotion. This could range from developing incentive programs that promise postgraduation employment for students who complete certain coursework or technical training to providing tax incentives to corporations that provide financial

6. For details of tax exemptions and one overseas book-distribution program, see the Sabre Foundation, http://www.sabre.org.

support to book-purchasing initiatives, English-language programs, or scholarship funds in their local overseas communities.

Even a long list of initiatives such as this (and the list could be much longer) will only touch a relatively small number of students at all ages. But just as Islamists enjoy a reputation for providing efficient social welfare services far beyond the actual reach of people that receive such services, so, too, will the example of successful English-language programming attract admirers far beyond the actual number of students that directly benefit from it. And along the way, the United States will have invested in the next generation of Muslim allies to carry on the campaign to limit the appeal of Islamism.

A Diplomacy of Doing

There is a tendency to see public diplomacy as mainly talking: whether through radio broadcasts, speaker programs, or print publications and the like. That is about as inadequate a view of public diplomacy as demarching foreign governments is of traditional diplomacy. To be effective, public diplomacy requires action—assertive, aggressive, creative efforts to engage foreign publics, nurture friends, empower allies, build future supporters, and undercut the leverage of America's adversaries. To succeed against as wily and sophisticated a challenge as Islamism requires resorting to means not usually the hallmark of traditional diplomacy. These means include more public-private partnerships, for example, and the encouragement of a more entrepreneurial, risk-taking, opportunistic, and decentralized way of doing business by America's embassies and diplomats.

This, in turn, will require changes from the current pattern

of foreign service recruitment, education, training, and place-
ment. Indeed, to a great extent, a successful public diplomacy
campaign against Islamism means a throwback to the days
before all diplomacy was directed from Washington, to the era
when embassies and diplomats were active, frontline agents
in the advance of American national interests. Only a diplomatic corps imbued with mission, charged with action, and
unleashed from bureaucracy can win the friends and allies
America needs to triumph in the battle to curtail the appeal of
Islamism.

Last
Exhibit

16

Anti-Americanism, U.S. Foreign Policy, and the War on Terrorism

Adam Garfinkle

To the extent that those who do not like America admit the fact, nearly all contend that the reason lies not with them but with and within America. A few such persons go beyond dislike to hatred, and a few of those go from passive to active expressions of that hatred. A few of those active expressions are violent, and a few of those, if they randomly target civilians, are terrorist. And a very few of those, if they cross trend lines with WMD proliferation, are arguably the most dangerous national security threat facing America today.

Now, if anti-Americanism is really the fault of the United States, if American policies justify the hatred of others toward the United States, then it follows logically that we can eliminate the terrorist threat if and only if we change our policies. If that is true, then all our exertions at public diplomacy, all our efforts to understand the sociology of the Arab and Mus-

This chapter reflects the author's own views and does not represent the views of the U.S. government or the Department of State.

lim worlds, all our labors to liberalize the political cultures of the Middle East are pointless and futile. If such a view were true, it would be very important to know it, because such knowledge could save us an enormous amount of time, money, and misplaced expectations. Armed with such knowledge, we could simply economically change the bad policies with dispatch, and that, presumably, would be that.

A good example of that very view is exemplified in a fairly recent article by Lamis Andoni, a Jordanian journalist who is by no means a radical, a terrorist, or an irrational hysteric. This well-known and well-respected Arab journalist is sure that American policies "perpetuate inequities and exacerbate regional conflicts," which is a code phrase, of course, for America's support for Israel. That support is why, Andoni claims, "neither U.S. control over the flow of news, nor the efforts of Pentagon and Madison Avenue spin doctors, can ease the resentment of U.S. policies and actions that have affected the lives, hearts, and minds of the people of the region."

More than that, Andoni is "alarmed" that "the United States fails to realize that a foreign policy based solely on such principles of power and domination leave no room for legitimate political opposition, driving all discontent into the camp of extremists and terrorists."[1] Hence the conclusion, so widespread even among those who do not hate America, that we "deserved" what we got on September 11, 2001. We presumably deserved what we got because we exacerbate conflicts,

---

1. Lamis Andoni, "Deeds Speak Louder Than Words," in *The Battle for Hearts and Minds: Using Soft Power to Undermine Terrorist Networks*, ed. Alexander T.J. Lennon (Cambridge, MA: MIT Press, 2003), 262–63. A similar account of Muslim/Indonesian views may be gleaned from Jane Perlez, "U.S. Asks Muslims Why It Is Unloved. Indonesians Reply," *New York Times*, September 27, 2003; and Pakistani views from Hussein Haqqaqi, "The Rage of Moderate Islam," *Foreign Policy*, January/February 2004, 74–76. Haqqaqi reviews Khurshid Ahmed's *Amrika: Luslim Dunya ki Bey-Itminani* ("America and Unrest in the Muslim World") (Islamabad: Institute of Policy Studies, 2002).

and we are responsible for authoritarian Arab and Muslim governments that repress all dissent and force people to extremism and terrorism. Our victimhood, in short, is all our own fault.

Those who believe this line of argument are thoroughly unconcerned about the principles and interests that might be adversely affected by abrupt and major changes in U.S. policy. They are unconcerned for one, or both, of two reasons. The first reason is the assumption that there would *be* no adverse effects—that policies that deserve to be hated ought to be changed, terrorism or no terrorism. The second is that no principle or interest could be as important as eliminating the threat of mass-casualty terrorism that confronts America.

If the situation is really so simple and clear-cut, why, then, do such supposedly terrible and counterproductive U.S. policies persist as they do? Many abroad, and some in the United States, who take this point of view have a handy explanation: because U.S. policy is in thrall to a powerful domestic lobby— the Jews.[2] It never occurs to most such people that the president and those of his cabinet members who are relevant to foreign policy—none of whom are Jews—might have good reasons, fully in the U.S. national interest, for the policies they determine. Were these people to acknowledge such reasons, however, it would mean that their own views were not so obviously justified after all. So, those who hold such views of the origins of U.S. policies instead prefer explanations based on plots and conspiracies because those explanations are so easy on the brain and are so comforting to preconceived biases.

Not a single element of what we may call the Andoni et al.

---

2. A popular example in a European context is Michael Lind, "The Israel Lobby," *Prospect* (April 2002). My rebuttal may be found in "The Israel Lobby— Part II," *Prospect* (September 2002). In the United States, almost any issue of Patrick Buchanan's magazine *The American Conservative* will display an example.

argument is correct. Only some anti-Americanism is a function of American policy, and the most dangerous kind linked to terrorism really is not (of which, more below). Changing good, reasonable policies under the pressure of terrorist threats would not make us safer. To the contrary, it would unleash a feeding frenzy of pressure on American interests worldwide. A self-interested, parochial cabal does not control American foreign policy against the national interest. Nor is it true, as always implied if not always stated, that U.S. support for Israel is really at the top of every Arab and Muslim's agenda, despite the efforts of al-Jazeera's electronic yellow journalism to make it so.[3] And American foreign policy is most certainly *not* based solely on "principles of power and domination."

For what it may be worth, the United States is also not responsible for the rise of authoritarian government in the Middle East. Such authoritarianism was firmly in place long before American influence arrived on the scene, and our capacity to change it today is much more limited than many think. In addition, the very same people who chastise us for intervening imperially into affairs that are supposedly none of our business are often the first ones to urge us to intervene into the affairs of those they dislike and wish to constrain or harm.

But because the general story line sketched above is so widely believed in the Middle East, and increasingly in Europe, public diplomacy and other "soft" instruments of

3. It certainly is not a big concern in post-Ba'athi Iraq, to take one important example. Ambassador Hume Horan was attached to the Coalition Provisional Authority in Baghdad, from which he traveled the country for several months, having hundreds of conversations with Iraqis from all walks of life. "I've been here four months," Ambassador Horan wrote to me, "and *no one has ever raised the Palestinians or the Arab-Israeli issue with me. Stale Arab causes are in the doghouse these days.*" E-mail communication, September 4, 2003 (emphasis in original).

American policy are necessary and important and can surely do some good if wisely employed.

Of course, there are limits. We will never convince most of our enemies that their addled, paranoid, conspiratorial way of seeing the world is mistaken, and we must still do what we think is right, even if others misunderstand our motives for doing it. The clearest and most unapologetic articulation of this truth is that of Fouad Ajami:

> There should be no illusions about the sort of Arab landscape that America is destined to find if, or when, it embarks on a war against the Iraqi regime. There would be no "hearts and minds" to be won in the Arab world, no public diplomacy that would convince the overwhelming majority of Arabs that this war would be a just war. An American expedition in the wake of thwarted UN inspections would be seen by the vast majority of Arabs as an imperial reach into their world, a favor to Israel, or a way for the United States to secure control over Iraq's oil. No hearing would be given to the great foreign power.
>
> America ought to be able to live with this distrust and discount a good deal of this anti-Americanism as the "road rage" of a thwarted Arab world—the congenital condition of a culture yet to take full responsibility for its self-inflicted wounds. There is no need to pay excessive deference to the political pieties and givens of the region.[4]

All of this is true enough. But that misunderstanding, as pervasive as it is, is an autonomous factor—it is part of our problem, and not, all things considered, a small part. We *can* convince some in the Middle East that this story line is wrong, not least because it *is* wrong. We have to try. To try, however, we need a more sophisticated understanding of anti-Americanism and of a growing Middle Eastern anti-Semitism that is closely related to it.

4. Fouad Ajami, "Iraq and the Arabs' Future," *Foreign Affairs* (January–February 2003).

The Nature of Anti-Americanism

There is loose in the world a perception of sharply rising anti-Americanism. That perception resides not least in the minds of many newspaper and journal editors and sundry other intellectuals, both in the United States and abroad. The frequent repetition of this perception bears influence in its own right, whether or not the facts match the perception—and to a considerable extent, they don't.

Let's be honest: much of the commentary on rising anti-Americanism presumes a cause—the supposed arrogance, self-absorption, and unilateralism of the George W. Bush administration. Those members of the "commentariat" who accept this characterization of the U.S. administration often begin with a conclusion that then presumes to sire its own factual premise.[5]

The actual facts say otherwise. True, there has been an increase in anti-Americanism in the past few years, and there has been a sharp spike corresponding to the period of the war in Iraq. But the increase has not been nearly as great as the commentariat typically suggests, and the reasons for the increase are more varied than usually averred. So says not only the U.S. Department of State's global opinion monitors but also a host of private professional polling and opinion analysis organizations.

Of course, measuring opinion is notoriously difficult, even in one's own country. It is harder still in countries with different attitudes toward the press and the common weal in general. Establishing the reasons that people express the opinions they do is harder still (of which also, more below). The begin-

5. A similar argument is advanced by Secretary of State Colin L. Powell in *The Economist*'s special issue, "The World in 2004" (January 2004): 66.

ning of wisdom in making one's way through this thorny topic is recognizing that distinctions matter. Anti-Americanism is, in truth, not one phenomenon but several.

Some people loathe the very idea of America. Even after "the end of history," in Francis Fukuyama's famous phrase, there are those who disparage the institutions of constitutional liberalism, who deprecate democracy, and who despise free-market economies. There are still many outside the zone of Western culture who equate liberty with license and equality under the law with the violation of some imagined hierarchy thought to inhere in nature itself. Opposition to America as an idea is an old prejudice indeed, going back to the very founding of the Republic. One may call it *philosophical* anti-Americanism.

Others do not like what they know of American culture, which inundates many societies these days without asking the permission of their elders. Not everyone likes popular cultural artifacts that are steeped in vulgarity, disrespect for elders and teachers, and countless variations on puerile promiscuity; even in the United States, there are a few of us left who feel the same way. We see, however, that freedom entails the right of others to debase themselves, and we know that we need not join their clubs if we do not wish to do so. But many abroad miss this subtlety. One may call their distate *cultural* anti-Americanism.

Still others like neither the particular policies of the American government nor the key personalities in a particular American administration. We may call this *contingent* anti-Americanism.

Sometimes philosophical, cultural, and contingent forms of anti-Americanism overlap. Often, however, they do not. Nor are these three varieties or facets of anti-Americanism evenly distributed around the world. The data show the sharpest contemporary anti-Americanism to be concentrated in two groups; but, as we will see, these groups do not much share the same kind of anti-Americanism.

The first of these groups is large: average citizens in most Arab and many majority-Muslim societies. Anti-Americanism is often expressed in these societies in terms of particular policies: toward the Arab-Israeli conflict, toward the stationing of U.S. military forces in the region, and, until spring 2003, toward the sanctions regime against Iraq (and since then toward the American "occupation" of Iraq). Many people in the Arab and Muslim worlds distinguish between America and the American people on the one hand, and the American government on the other. This distinction is why it is really not so hard to understand why the same people who publicly excoriate America in one breath are often eager to express a desire to visit, work, and even immigrate to the United States in the next.

Not all Arab and Muslim anti-Americanism is of the contingent sort. Certainly, the supporters of Osama bin Laden are possessed of a rabid philosophical anti-Americanism. But in between the typical man on the street and the Islamist ideologue is a growing cultural anti-Americanism.

In this era of information technology diffusion, cultural anti-Americanism is spreading worldwide. So too, oddly enough as it would seem, is the popularity of American mass-market culture—rock music, jeans, backward baseball caps, and the rest. This seeming contradiction is not a contradiction at all, however. The fact is that rapid social change, accelerated by the information revolution, has produced a huge generation gap in many traditional and transitional societies. The young abroad tend to anathematize American policies while embracing American styles. Older people tend to anathematize American styles, regardless of what they may think and feel about American policies.

America's image in the world, popular or not, is seriously distorted by our pop cultural extrusions. The source of the distortion exists, in part, because Hollywood and the American advertising culture export images of America abroad that do not match American social realities.

Several studies—including many directed by Dr. George Gerbner at the University of Pennsylvania's Annenberg School of Communications—have shown, for example, that characters on network television are at least *fifty* times more likely to fall victim to acts of violence than the citizens of the real America. Violence is even more prevalent in exports of American television shows and movies, for the simple reason that the main expense in preparing a film for export is the cost of translation, whether dubbing or writing subtitles. The richer and more subtle the dialogue and plot, the harder and more costly the translation. Explosions and gunfire, alas, do not require translation, so films rich in such pyrotechnics are usually cheaper to export, hence more profitable for the studios.

In American entertainment exports, depictions of sex outside marriage are nine to fourteen times more common than dramatizations of marital sex. This is a fictional proportionality, one can safely assume, that is wildly out of whack with the real America. It would be wildly out of whack even with the real France, Italy, and Germany. One hopes so, anyway.

For better *and* for worse, there is little the U.S. government can do about America's entertainment industry exports. However, the cumulative impact of those exports on how America is seen and judged outside our borders is not so small. This is particularly so in parts of the world where traditional religious attitudes toward sexuality remain intact—in other words, where they resemble attitudes almost universally held in the United States until only a few generations ago. (It is very important for Americans to realize that the values gap between American society and societies like those of Iran and Egypt has been produced not by recent changes in Iran and Egypt but by recent changes in America.)

The second major focus of contemporary anti-Americanism is much smaller in terms of the number of people involved: certain groups of intellectuals, mainly in Europe. But the influence of a small number of intellectuals is not thereby small. Ideas, even bad ones, have power. For these groups, disenchantment with American policies is more the pretext for an anti-Americanism that is philosophically deep-seated. This philosophical anti-Americanism has an old pedigree in resentment of a free and socially freewheeling America by the conservative, aristocratic blue bloods of Europe.

That such a prejudice, in somewhat modified form, has spread to the European Left over the past half-century is an ironic and interesting development. This spread can be seen in the recent book by Emmanuel Todd, *Après l'Empire: Essai sur la décomposition du système américain*, which was enormously popular and influential in France, and elsewhere in Europe, just before and during the war in Iraq. However, Todd, who describes America as the "singular threat to global stability weighing on the world today," has not been able to overtake the popularity of Michael Moore in Germany. *"Stupid White Men": Eine Abrechnung dem Amerika unter George W. Bush* has been, by far, the best-selling item of its kind in German translation. This anti-administration diatribe has sold well over a million copies and was on the German best-seller list for more than forty weeks running in 2002 and 2003. For several weeks in spring 2003, it topped the list. As of this writing, Moore's book has sold *more copies in German* than has the original

English-language edition in North America, where the market is far larger.

Moore's film *Bowling for Columbine* has also been very popular in Germany; about a million people have viewed it to date, according to sources in the U.S. embassy in Berlin. Touted as a true-to-life depiction of America's violent culture, some German middle and high school teachers have proclaimed mandatory field trips to take students to see it. As Fred Kempe of the *European Wall Street Journal* put it, it cannot be without some significance (significance for Germany, not for the United States) that Michael Moore is the most popular American in Germany.

In Germany, and elsewhere in western Europe, cultural and contingent anti-Americanism have clearly mixed with and helped spread philosophical anti-Americanism during the past two years. Whether this new mixture will "take," however, and give rise to a new anti-American reality in Europe remains an open question. Most likely it won't, at least not among typical Europeans. Among *Muslims* living in Europe, however, it is another matter.

Outside of these two groups—the Arab/Muslim domain and a small group of European intellectuals—recent increases in anti-Americanism are either modest or nonexistent. One highly respected survey, the Pew Global Attitudes Project (PGAP), put it this way in 2002: "While criticism of America is on the rise, a reserve of goodwill toward the United States still remains." The United States and its citizens were positively rated by majorities in thirty-five out of forty-two countries in the PGAP survey.

It is worth recalling, too, that recent increases in anti-Americanism have followed a period, after September 11, 2001, in which sympathy for the United States spiked up in most regions and countries. Increased anti-Americanism has also come in train with two U.S.-led wars, in Afghanistan and Iraq, that took place within a relatively short period. Clearly, the need for the United States to respond with military force to the events of September 11 inevitably magnified the perception of American "hard" power in a way that has made many people abroad uncomfortable.

Nonetheless, despite these special circumstances, the level of ill will for the United States expressed in the past two to three years is not markedly different from that expressed five or ten or twenty years ago. We have not, therefore, witnessed a deepening groundswell of hatred for the United States. In addition, it is very likely that the increases we have witnessed with the Iraq War will subside in due course, notably in Europe. Indeed, some recent data suggest that they already are.

Beyond media exaggerations, the perception of a sharp rise in anti-Americanism owes much to a key misperception among many Americans. The terrorist attacks of September 11 surprised most Americans, as well as frightened them. As the spate of "Why do they hate us?" press features illustrated, most Americans were not aware of much anti-American resentment in the world until it issued forth in large-scale murder on U.S. soil. As a rule, Americans are fairly informal and friendly people. Unless given a reason not to, they are inclined to like other peoples, and they expect other peoples to like them. Our citizens have been disturbed to learn that not everyone does like Americans, and this sudden awareness has led many to overestimate now what they underestimated before.

Other sorts of dynamics affect opinion and polling outside the United States. Some of what gets counted as anti-Americanism is not always as it seems. Anti-Americanism in some Middle Eastern climes has an almost allegorical character to it.

In authoritarian political cultures, the average person is often reluctant to answer pollsters' questions honestly. In some of those cultures, too, citizens may be tempted to deflect frustration with their own government and society by blaming America. After all, America is far away, and it will not send goons with guns and billy clubs to knock on the door in the middle of the night.

Some authoritarian governments, justifiably frightened of their own people's wrath, actively encourage such deflectionary anti-Americanism in their official press. Many such governments have systematically been doing this for years, and some, amazingly, still claim to be true allies of the United States. If asked for a political opinion by a pollster, typical respondents stuck in such an information environment may say what they think their government wants them to say. They may believe their own answers, or they may not; it is almost impossible to know. Either way, toeing the official line is a way to stay out of trouble and to please those who control status, jobs, and access to credit.

The genealogy of Europe's philosophical anti-Americanism, on the other hand, has nothing to do with allegory. As James W. Ceaser pointed out in the summer 2002 issue of *The Public Interest*, in the late eighteenth century, many educated Europeans believed that the climate of America was prone to creating degeneracy and monstrosity in all living things. The Count de Buffon originated this preposterous thesis, which was taken up and popularized by Cornelius de Pauw. Thomas Jefferson took pains in his only book, *Notes on the State of Virginia*, to debunk it.

In the nineteenth century, European anti-Americanism focused on opposition to the universalist principles of American public life. Many anti-Americans were romantics who found in America an excess of rationalism and who excoriated

America for having no real culture or history and no noteworthy national bloodline. What America did have, as many European intellectuals from privileged classes saw it, was a dangerous obsession with leveling of all kinds.

From Joseph de Maistre to Heinrich Heine, this anti-American view dominated European intellectual life for decades and it was joined toward the end of the nineteenth century by a more explicitly racist element. Americans were racially impure and hence degenerate, said Arthur de Gobineau, the inventor, it so happens, of modern "scientific" anti-Semitism. This idea was more widespread than one would like nowadays to think. (The association of anti-Semitism with anti-Americanism has precedent, by the way: much anti-British sentiment during the heyday of British power, when London epitomized modernity and rationality, was also heavily laden with anti-Semitism, as the rantings of John Atkinson Hobson illustrate.)

In the twentieth century, anti-Americanism joined with newer streams of antimodernism. As Ceaser points out, not a small number of European intellectuals loathed standardized industrial production and were deeply suspicious of "culture for the masses." Thus, for example, Friedrich Nietzsche and Rainer Marie Rilke's intense dislike of America. The term *Americanization* was coined to mean turning true culture and spirit into base materialism. Thus, the influential view of Martin Heidegger, who started as a Nazi sympathizer but whose fulminations subsequently infused the postwar European Left through Jean-Paul Sartre and others. As prelude to Europe's Luddite-like antiglobalization movement of our own time, to the thinking of Emmanuel Todd as well as Jose Bové, this legacy of European thought finds its place.

The Old-New Anti-Semitism

Obviously, there are many people in the Arab and Muslim worlds who are in no way anti-American. Obviously, too, most Europeans do not share the prejudices of a segment of their intellectual elite. Even so, anti-Americanism is a problem, not least because, as noted at the outset, a small number of people are motivated to translate their prejudice into violence. What is interesting, but also worrisome, is the coming together of strains of both anti-Americanism and anti-Semitism among radicalized Muslims born in Europe.

Olivier Roy's analysis points to a rich and varied Muslim sociology in western Europe. Roy has given thought, in passing in this volume and in greater length elsewhere, to the possibility that radical Islam in Europe might ally with radical left-wing movements (and maybe even radical right-wing movements). If so, the rabid anti-Semitism of both would serve as an anchor of common belief.

Roy has also pointed out that radical Muslims really come in two different categories. There are local or regional radicals, whose targets tend to be all that they define as alien to Islam in their midst: Jews and foreigners and the locals who "serve" them. For example, recent attacks in Morocco, Turkey, Saudi Arabia, and elsewhere were aimed not at local residents or even at government targets, such as police or political figures; instead, they were aimed at synagogues, foreign consulates, and restaurants and facilities where nonresidents congregate. In the Saudi case of November 2003, the attacks were aimed at non-Saudi Arabs.

The other category Roy (and others) defines as internationalist. These are mostly Arabs who live in the West, speak a Western language, lack a formal Islamic religious education, and have taken a Western academic program. Most have been radicalized in Europe; some are immigrants, but most are European-born. Many do not speak Arabic or any Middle Eastern language. In the course of their radicalization, they break with their families and, indeed, with traditional Islamic and diaspora traditions. These are rootless internationalist radicals, who were followers of Sayyid Qutb before they were followers of Osama bin Laden. Their aim is to strike at the source of the humiliation and powerlessness of Islam—the West, led by the United States.

Such radicals have one foot in the West and one in an idealist Islam that lacks genuine Middle Eastern roots. They are a modern, or postmodern, phenomenon of deculturation under the pressures of globalization. Their methods, too, are modern, and their aims have little to do with the Middle East. Roy points out that the favorite destinations for jihad of Muslim internationalists are at the periphery of the Muslim world: Chechnya, Bosnia, Kashmir, and New York. There are no examples of people like Muhammad Atta returning to their or their family's country of origin to engage in jihad.

These radicals, the most dangerous international terrorists, do not care about parochial conflicts in Algeria, Egypt, or Palestine. Osama bin Laden's *fatwa* against Jews and crusaders was issued when the Oslo process appeared to be going fine. If they hate Ariel Sharon, they hated Ehud Barak no less. The contention that a settlement of the Israeli-Palestinian conflict would have a significant positive effect on the kind of threat al Qaeda poses to the United States is therefore completely false.

A solution to that conflict would be a good thing, of course, for several other reasons. But any solution with which the United States would be involved would obviously leave Israel as a Jewish state in one set of borders or another. In return for that, the Palestinian Authority would have to agree to end the conflict short of totally recovering all of historical, geographical Palestine. If the Palestinians as a whole accept that sort of compromise, most Arabs and most Muslims would accept it, too. But some would not. Muslim radicals would see any Palestinian who agreed to such a settlement just as Istambuli saw Sadat: as an apostate from true Islam who deserves to be killed. Even among local Islamists, the prospect of such a settlement could be expected to increase terrorism, not reduce it, at least in the short term.

Such a settlement's impact on al Qaeda terrorists would probably not be very significant. But any impact it would have would most likely lead to *more* terrorism, against the United States, not less, for its having sponsored or mediated such an unacceptable settlement. The fact is that when most Arabs and Muslims argue that U.S. policy unfairly tilts in favor of Israel, they do not mean that the United States emboldens and supports Israel's occupation of territories taken in the June 1967 war. Rather, they refer to "occupied Palestinian territories," which to most means all of Palestine. Over the years, the Arab media, official and otherwise, have peddled a truly demonic image of Israel—state, society, ideology, everything. Israel sterilizes Egyptian women by putting secret ingredients in chewing gum. Israel deliberately spreads AIDS to the Arabs. Israelis kill Arab children to bake their blood into matzos for Passover. An extraordinary number of Arabs actually believe that such utter nonsense is true.

With such demonization has come a European-imported "literary" anti-Semitism circa the 1930s, complete with popular Arabic versions of *The Protocols of the Elders of Zion*.[6] The way

6. See Robert S. Wistrich, "The Old-New Anti-Semitism," *The National Interest*, no. 72 (Summer 2003).

Israel has been depicted makes the idea of peace and normalization with it virtually unthinkable to most Arabs—except, ironically, to many Palestinians, who actually have some degree of personal familiarity with Israel.

Given this "vision" of what Israel is, which is very widely shared from Morocco to Indonesia, no imaginable American-sponsored compromise settlement could erase the contention that American policy is one-sided, unfair, perpetuates inequities, and so forth. Indeed, for America to be truly liked these days in much of the Arab and Muslim worlds, American society and policy would have to become as routinely and as matter-of-factly anti-Semitic as theirs. Happily, this is not very likely.

The issue of Palestine has special resonance in the Arab and Muslim worlds for several reasons. One is that it is the quintessential pan-Islamic issue, largely because of the status of the Haram al-Sharif, the area in Jerusalem containing the al-Aqsa Mosque and the Dome of the Rock. In addition, Palestine is a collective symbol of Arab humiliation, particularly so at the hands of the Jews, who don't come out too well in the Qur'an.

However, the Palestine issue is one that works only at the high symbolic level. It has nothing to do with borders, security arrangements, water rights, and all the other elements in dispute that Western analysts, casual and otherwise, spend almost all their time trying to figure out. Most Arabs and Muslims in countries that have no border with Israel are almost completely ignorant of the state of play on such discrete issues and couldn't care less about them. All they know is that Israel is illegitimate, occupies holy Jerusalem, and is an anti-Islamic spearhead of the Christian West—a message whose resonance comes from the continued perseveration on Western colonialism in these societies. Failing elites deploy such a fixation to explain (away) the pathetic state of most of these countries.[7]

In short, those who see an imposed solution to the Israeli-Palestinian/Arab conflict as a U.S. strategic imperative because of the general context of the war on terrorism are mistaken about every one of their premises. If the United States were to pressure a democratic ally to make concessions to Islamist terrorism, it would be open season on U.S. interests wherever those interests touch the Muslim world. India, Russia, China, and other non-Muslim countries that share borders with Islam, either internally or externally, would come to regret such a decision, too.

It is true, however, that America supports Israel and that, because of Israel's wildly distorted image in the Arab and Muslim worlds, America suffers by association. What can be done about this?

As Ajami suggests, not much can be done, soon or directly. Ironically, the best way to go at this problem would be for Palestinian Arabs to become truth-tellers to the rest of the Arab and Muslim world. That could happen if Palestinians and Israelis, on their own, not by imposition, could arrive at a stable compromise peace. This is possible; it is even likely over the next half dozen years. Then it might be possible for Jordanians and Egyptians to get to know the real Israel better; the anti-Israel and anti-Semitic stereotypes so prevalent in the region might become weakened over time through Palestinian, Egyptian, and Jordanian media and word-of-mouth. In other words, if there is peace, reality will eventually intrude on lurid fantasy. In the meantime, there is a real limit to what

---

7. See the excellent analysis on this point of Michael Doran, "Palestine, Iraq and American Strategy," *Foreign Affairs* (January–February 2002).

American public diplomacy can achieve, particularly official, government-sponsored public diplomacy.

Last Words

A certain amount of anti-Americanism is inevitable. It goes with the territory of being number one in terms of raw military, political, and economic clout. The United States did not actively seek such a global status. Gideon Rose put it well: "America's role in international affairs today is not a sign of a quest for power, but a reflection of it."[8] But it doesn't matter how we got to be number one. There will always be those who fear the power of others, no matter the disposition of those who control that power. There will always be those whose capacity for envy exceeds their capacity for appreciation. It is as Machiavelli said: "Men's hatreds generally spring from fear and envy." That means, these days, that the potential for terrorism based in anti-Americanism can probably never be eliminated completely, only controlled and managed.

Although a certain amount of anti-Americanism does come with the territory of great power status, the U.S. government has no business making an unfortunate situation worse. Those in government must be sensitive to the tone of their pronouncements, more so now than ever in the past: As U.S. power waxes, so must its sense of restraint and responsibility. American policy makers must exercise forethought as to how actions, even when taken with the most benevolent of motives, may be seen by others.

This means that public diplomacy functions must be taken more seriously. American officials can no longer assume, as

8. Gideon Rose, "Imperialism: The Highest State of American Capitalism?" *The National Interest*, no. 71 (Spring 2003).

has historically been their inclination, that the truth about American intentions will be obvious to everyone, or at least to everyone who matters. This is particularly true in regard to people in societies without access to free media and in which conspiracy theories are often accepted as matters of fact. Official American public diplomacy must do a much better job at monitoring falsehood and incitement, talking back to it, and unapologetically explaining American policies. As the Djerejian Report insists, we need to spend more money—a lot more money—to do this right.[9]

But getting at the broader cultural side of the problem is, as Ellen Laipson argues, no longer a job for government.[10] This function is very important, but it needs to be privatized. American and international foundations should be set up for such purposes, and those already in existence need to be quietly supported. Government can help coordinate some of these activities, encourage them with tax breaks, and help make sure the basic message is consistent with government policy. But any more direct role than that for government is the kiss of death as long as America's image remains as sullied, justifiably or not, as it is today. That is why the general "new" approach of Radio Sawa and Radio Farda is unfortunate; these media outlets are examples of approaches that ought to be in the private sector.[11] It is also why the U.S. government–run Al

9. *Changing Minds, Winning Peace: A New Strategic Direction for U.S. Public Diplomacy in the Arab and Muslim World* (Washington, D.C.: Advisory Group on Public Diplomacy in the Muslim World, October 1, 2003): 25–26.

10. See also Michael Holtzman, "Privatize Public Diplomacy" and "Selling America to the Muslims," *New York Times*, August 8, 2002, and October 7, 2003, respectively.

11. Radio Sawa isn't working. See, for example, Duraid al-Baik, "Media Battle Rages on Air to Win Over Arab Minds," *Arab News* (Dubai), (November 11, 2003).

Hurra Arabic satellite television station, based in Springfield, Virginia, is likely to be a failure and a waste of money.[12]

The distinction between government and private sector efforts is important; but there is another distinction that bears stressing, or repeating. To the extent that anti-Americanism is based on honest disagreement with American philosophy or policies, Americans, in government and out, should accept it and learn to live with it. In some cases, some Americans see anti-Americanism where there is only honest disagreement with a policy choice. Americans who cannot distinguish between those who hate Americans and those who disagree on the merits with the policy choices of the American government are liable to cause more anti-Americanism than they can possibly identify.

But to the extent that anti-Americanism is based on irrational premises that spring from social-political dysfunction abroad, we need to unmask and contend with that irrationality and dysfunction. Americans are, by and large, open to rational persuasion, and sometimes we are persuaded. But the American government should not, and will not, alter policies it knows to be correct just to please those who threaten the United States. It certainly will not bend before those who defame and impugn the United States from pathologies of their own making. After all, as many a wit has pointed out, it can be an honor to be hated, if one is hated by the right sort of people.

12. See Jim Rutenberg, "Coming Soon to Arab TVs: U.S. Answer to Al Jazeera, Production Values and All," *New York Times*, December 27, 2003.

Index